Enough

Enough

Why It's Time to Abolish the Super-Rich

Luke Hildyard

First published 2024 by Pluto Press
New Wing, Somerset House, Strand, London WC2R 1LA
and Pluto Press, Inc.
1930 Village Center Circle, 3-834, Las Vegas, NV 89134

www.plutobooks.com

British Library Cataloguing in Publication Data
A catalogue record for this book is available from the British Library

ISBN   978 0 7453 4854 4   Paperback
ISBN   978 0 7453 4855 1   PDF
ISBN   978 0 7453 4856 8   EPUB

This book is printed on paper suitable for recycling and made from
fully managed and sustained forest sources. Logging, pulping and
manufacturing processes are expected to conform to the environmental standards of the country of origin.

Typeset by Stanford DTP Services, Northampton, England

Simultaneously printed in the United Kingdom and United States of
America

Contents

Acknowledgements

This book draws particularly on work done by the High Pay Centre, and I would especially like to thank colleagues behind a lot of the research and arguments cited – Andrew Speke, Rachel Kay, Harry Window and Rosie Neville.

The book also cites a number of external studies from other academics and researchers and I'm very grateful to authors who took time to discuss their work with me and highlight other relevant research, including Arun Advani, Andy Summers, Karen Rowlingson, Alex Maitland, Beth Stratford, Robert Palmer, Paul Monaghan, Thomas Dudley, Ethan Rouen and Camille Landais.

I am particularly grateful to David Castle at Pluto Press for commissioning the book and providing really useful insights and comments on drafts, as well as to Robert Webb during the production process, to Sophie Richmond for copy-editing, Dave Stanford and Melanie Patrick for design and formatting and to other Pluto colleagues involved with promotion and marketing: Emily Orford, Chris Browne, Alex Diamond-Rivlin, James Kelly, Jonila Krasniqi and Patrick Hughes.

Finally, I'd like to thank my incredible partner Georgina for being so unbelievably patient and supportive while I embarked on what was, with hindsight, the somewhat cavalier undertaking of writing a book while also trying to manage a full-time job and co-parent a one-year-old child.

Introduction: Our Passive Acceptance of the Super-Rich

As Director of the High Pay Centre, a 'think tank' that carries out research on economic inequality, employment rights and responsible business, I very occasionally get invited onto obscure radio stations at anti-social hours to join discussions on topics like CEO pay, bankers' bonuses or billionaire wealth, if ever they happen to be in the news. The High Pay Centre generally takes a critical view of inequality and the super-rich, so the conversations often also include a representative of a think tank or pressure group that thinks these issues don't matter so much. This ensures a balance of perspectives and if both of us tell friends or family we're appearing it probably helps to get the audience numbers into double figures.

On one such occasion the 'free market' activist responding to my comments about the need to curb executive pay suggested to me, the presenter and possibly some people listening at home that 'you don't make the poor richer by making the rich poorer'.[1] This comment summed up their argument with a line that was clear, memorable, effective and – in my opinion – profoundly wrong. In some ways, reflecting on that axiom, and the extent to which it shapes economic policy, and therefore people's standards of living, was the genesis of this book.

My instant response was to garble something profoundly forgettable and very 'think tank' about how policies and regulations that affect the distribution of economic resources are in fact vitally important determinants of living standards. The audience no doubt drifted into the next segment with the lasting impression that you don't make the poor richer by making the rich poorer.

To make the poor richer, you have to make the rich poorer

I should have just said 'yes you do'. There are already loads of ways in which money is taken from the rich and given to the poor, often mandated by government intervention. These can be grouped into two categories – 'redistribution', whereby the resources accumulated by the rich are transferred to those who are not so rich, and 'pre-distribution', meaning mechanisms that apply further upstream, preventing money or assets that would otherwise accrue to rich people from reaching them in the first place, and ensuring they flow to people who are less well-off instead. Both processes can affect levels of annual *income* (how much someone accumulates in a year) or *wealth* (the total value of their assets including property and other possessions, pensions or financial wealth).

Despite being the kind of exceptionally unpoetic terms only ever used by professional policymakers, redistribution and pre-distribution are critical to securing a decent standard of living for vast numbers of people. All countries already do both to differing extents, and poverty, inequality and instability would be much worse if they didn't.

Examples of redistribution include progressive taxes, which are paid disproportionately by rich people and used to benefit the entire population. This can mean literally giving money raised from the rich to the poor or disadvantaged – when these taxes are used to fund social security payments that support those on low incomes who might be in low-paying work, or have disabilities, or have lost their job. And it can also mean what is effectively indirect redistribution, whereby tax revenues are used to fund public services that benefit everyone – and that many people might otherwise be unable to afford – like health services or education.

Examples of pre-distribution include the minimum wage, which prohibits employers from paying their staff below a certain hourly rate, thus raising the pay of low earners and reducing the profits that would otherwise accrue to the business owners. Similarly, key employment rights, like rules guaranteeing trade union representation or preventing employers from sacking striking workers, are pre-distributive. They strengthen the negotiating position of generally lower-paid workers, meaning they get a bigger share of the revenues generated for the employer by their labour, again at the expense of profits accruing to the generally richer business owners.

In all these examples, the government makes poor people richer by making rich people poorer, either by giving the poorer people money or access to public services disproportionately paid for by rich people, or by implementing laws that facilitate increases to the income and wealth of generally poorer people at the expense of generally richer people.

Extreme high incomes and wealth sit alongside stagnating living standards and widespread hardship

The examples are interesting in the context of my talk radio interlocutor's comments, because all these developments – the welfare state funded through progressive taxation, the minimum wage and the role of trade unions in economic life – were considered to be bordering on revolution when they were originally proposed. But despite facing strong initial resistance, they are widely, if not universally, accepted (albeit to differing degrees) across all advanced economies by almost all mainstream political parties and are generally agreed to have hugely improved society.

Now, as of mid-2023, it is fairly uncontroversial to say that the UK is failing quite badly socio-economically in many different ways. After over 15 years of pay stagnation real average pay remains below 2008 levels.[2] Food bank use is hitting record highs.[3] Polling in spring 2023 suggested that around 5 million households could not afford to heat their homes adequately, while over 2 million had defaulted on major payments like their mortgage, rent or credit card bills in the previous month.[4]

Our public services and infrastructure are also in a parlous state. The number of people waiting for consultant-led treatment on the NHS had ballooned to over 7 million people by April 2023, with more than 4 million waiting for over 18 weeks, double the figure for those facing a similar wait in 2010.[5] An international analysis found that the UK has the fewest MRI/CT scanners of any of 19 comparable high-income countries, the second fewest hospital beds per 1,000 people and the fifth fewest intensive care beds.[6]

As these problems accumulate, the share of total incomes held by the richest 1 per cent of the UK population continues to hover close to its highest level since the Second World War, while the top 1 per cent by wealth own assets of a greater value than those of the bottom 50 per cent combined.[7] The combined wealth of the richest 350 households in Britain as reported by the Sunday Times Rich List reached a new high of nearly £800 billion in 2023.[8]

A similar contrast is visible in other countries. In the US, for example, the Institute for Policy Studies think tank estimated that between the outbreak of the Covid pandemic in March 2020 and autumn 2022 billionaire wealth increased by about 50 per cent or $5 trillion.[9]

At the same time, extraordinarily terrible developments are occurring regarding the health and well-being of millions of Americans. Life expectancy rates in the country have fallen, in part due to the pandemic, but also due to rising rates of suicide, drug overdoses and factors including alcoholism and poor diet.[10] In 2021, 210,000 Americans died from so-called 'deaths of despair', linked to alcohol abuse, drugs or suicide.[11]

An estimated 20 million people in the US are living in deep poverty – classified as having less than half the cash income required to surpass the poverty threshold (in 2021 this amounted to an income of less than $7,049 for a single individual under 65 and less than $13,740 for a family with two children).[12] Nearly 28 million Americans have no health insurance, meaning they potentially lack access to vital medical care.[13]

The problem of the Super-Rich is being ignored by politicians who think we can grow pies and cakes

Despite the juxtaposition of collapsing public services and widespread hardship on the one hand, and the inexhaustible accumulation of vast riches by a tiny number of already incredibly well-off people on the other, the potential to ameliorate socio-economic problems and generate wider well-being through redistribution or pre-distribution is essentially being ignored. It is extraordinary to record that in the political mainstream there is no real discussion of rebalancing income and wealth significantly, let alone a policy programme with that stated intent. The existence of the super-rich isn't seen as problematic or inefficient and the premise that to make the poor richer, you need to make the rich poorer is emphatically rejected, certainly by mainstream policymakers with any realistic prospect of political power.

Neither of the UK's two major political parties has, for example, committed to a wealth tax on millionaires that would generate billions in support of vital public services. Arguably the most high-profile reform the government has enacted since 'taking back control' of our laws from the EU on behalf of the left-behind regions of Britain was to lift the cap on bankers' bonuses.

It is true that the abolition of the top rate of income tax by the Liz Truss government in autumn 2022 was at least swiftly reversed, but the fact that the government's instinct was to *reduce* taxes on the very richest (and that plans to do so were wildly cheered by MPs in Parliament) demonstrates how far the prospect of significant *increases* in taxes on the rich remain from the mainstream.

Setting out her agenda as UK prime minister in the *Daily Mail*, Truss told readers that 'For too long politicians have fought over how to slice up the economic pie. My mission is to make it much bigger'.[14] This was one of the clearest expressions of a series of beliefs that have defined recent policymaking in the UK: a delusion that the country, one of the most unequal in the developed world, is overly focused on reducing inequality; a belief that distribution doesn't matter; and a bizarre conviction that this philosophy is best articulated via the medium of pie.

While the Truss premiership was famously unable to outlast the decomposition of a lettuce, these principles both pre-dated and have survived her. The Conservative MP Kemi Badenoch has also argued that 'for too long we have been focused on how we divide the pie' and advocated for growing it instead. She has risen, under Truss's successor Rishi Sunak, to become Secretary of State for Business and Trade, overseeing the policies and regulations affecting the pay practices of private sector employers and the millions of people who work for them.[15]

Her predecessor and fellow cabinet minister Grant Shapps, who evidently has more of a sweet tooth, was suggesting as long ago as 2014 that Labour was too fixated on how to divide the cake and never how to grow it.[16] In the run-up to the 2019 general election a co-author of the Conservative Party manifesto made more or less exactly the same point, again referring to cakes rather than pies, in a *Sunday Times* column.[17] Former prime minister Boris Johnson repeatedly emphasised that his levelling up agenda would not take resources from rich parts of the country and give them to poorer ones, insisting it was 'not a jam spreading exercise'.[18]

Cynics might say that these comments, and the image they evoke of Conservative ministers and advisers out in the garden of Downing Street attempting to 'grow' cakes and pies, rather explains the current state of the country. But they reflect a serious point about how trenchant opposition to sharing incomes and wealth more evenly is absolutely core to the identity of the modern Conservative Party.

At the same time, it is increasingly hard to understand who they define this view against. The comments from Grant Shapps implying that rebalancing the distribution of incomes and wealth is a priority for the centre left seems somewhat wide of the mark in 2023. While they make their point in a way that suggests they are less obsessed with picnics than their Tory counterparts, the substance of senior Labour Party figures' rhetoric on redistribution or pre-distribution is otherwise very similar.

For example, the Shadow Chancellor Rachel Reeves has emphasised that Labour would prefer to make society more equal by lifting people at the bottom up rather than bringing those at the top down (in reality, reducing inequality is likely to be more complicated than making a straightforward choice between these two options).[19] Other shadow cabinet ministers have argued that advocating greater equality undermines the party's efforts to be the party of aspiration, suggesting that they see some kind of contradiction between a more even balance of income and wealth and greater aggregate prosperity.[20] Labour has also explicitly ruled out introducing multiple taxes that would largely be borne by the super-rich, including a wealth tax, an increase in capital gains tax or a new top rate of income tax.[21]

The comments and commitments from politicians of both parties suggest a widespread view that there is no relationship between extreme riches at the top and hardship in the middle and at the bottom, and that redistribution and pre-distribution have little role to play in raising living standards. But while the economy is not a 'zero-sum game', whereby gains for one group mean equivalent losses for another, it would also be foolhardy to deny that there is sometimes competition over income or wealth, setting those at the top against those in the middle and at the bottom – for example, when businesses divide the revenue they generate between profits for their owners and wages for their workforce. Equally, there are multiple historical precedents – including, as previously noted, the establishment of trade unions during the Industrial Revolution, the creation of the NHS and the welfare state funded by progressive taxation or the introduction of the minimum wage – for using redistribution or pre-distribution to achieve giant improvements to people's lives. Given the scale of the incomes and wealth captured by the super-rich, and the difference that even a small fraction of this might make if shared more evenly with everybody else, politicians' failure to engage with these issues means that a big opportunity is being missed.

This cross-party consensus on tolerating extreme concentrations of income and wealth is again mirrored in America. The rhetoric towards the super-rich from Joe Biden as president has been different from that of centre-left counterparts in the UK. Biden has called for the wealthy to pay their fair share of taxes and proposed a 'billionaire tax' with a minimum taxation level for anyone with income of over $100 million. But the prospect of these proposals ever being realised, by politicians of either party, remains distant.

For many in America, opposition to any form of government intervention to redistribute or pre-distribute wealth, is couched more as an article of Taliban-style faith than a matter of socio-economic pragmatism – Biden's proposals to increase taxes on the rich have been repeatedly called 'un-American' by opponents, including by donors to the Democratic election campaign.[22] When the billionaire tax was initially mooted news channels reported little appetite from Democrat lawmakers for passing it.[23]

On the Republican side, the notion of mitigating inequality or rebalancing income and wealth distribution is treated as an enemy ideology – 'Socialism' or 'Marxism' designed to destroy America – rather than as an opposing view of how to make sensible economic policy that one might merely disagree with. The 2020 Conservative Political Action Conference adopted the tagline 'America versus Socialism' and proclaimed that unencumbered free enterprise was the work of God.[24] The former and potentially future president Donald Trump has even proposed that Socialists and Marxists should be banned from entering the country altogether.[25] Meanwhile, the prospect of any progressive changes to a situation whereby the richest 1 per cent of Americans by income have total incomes almost 50 per cent higher than the combined incomes of the poorest 50 per cent, and the richest 1 per cent by wealth control over a third of all household wealth, remains remote.[26]

The super-rich are tragically unloathed

Of course, while politicians need to be able to lead public opinion, their policy positions will always follow it to some extent. And this explains a great deal about the reluctance of political parties across the spectrum to view the super-rich as a problem that needs addressing, or to see redistribution and pre-distribution as a viable way of raising living standards. There is limited public appetite for such measures, and good grounds to think that they would prove actively unpopular.

It is true that opinion polls tend to show strong majorities in support of higher taxes on the rich or a cap on executive pay at a multiple of the lowest-paid employees.[27] But what survey respondents say they feel in isolation about an issue to which they have not given a lot of thought is very different to the reaction that the same policies spark as part of a broader programme in a 'real-world' environment, where they are being publicly debated and criticised by their most vehement opponents.

Probably the best example of this comes from the 2019 UK general election, when Labour did make redistribution and pre-distribution a key theme of the campaign and lost heavily. While Brexit and the leadership of Jeremy Corbyn were blamed as the critical factors, research has shown that these were intertwined with doubts about the feasibility of Labour's economic agenda.[28] In the context of Labour's current lack of interest in engaging with extreme concentrations of income and wealth, this rather underlines the point about political leaders following public opinion as much as leading it.

Subtler polling questions often reveal attitudes to the super-rich that are either more nuanced or intrinsically sympathetic and don't necessarily suggest a desire for meaningful rebalancing of income and wealth. When the Edelman Trust

Barometer asked how the UK government should deal with the cost of living crisis, 'increase taxes on the rich' was the most popular response selected from a list of options but 'address systemic injustice and discrimination' was the second least popular.[29] People understand that the super-rich can afford to make a significant tax contribution, but are much warier of the idea that we can and should fundamentally transform the economic system so that the incomes and wealth generated in the UK are more evenly and proportionately shared.

Public opinion research comparing attitudes internationally finds that in the UK together with the US, hostility towards the super-rich is comparatively limited. Survey respondents in Britain agreed that hard work generally leads to success by a margin of 57 per cent to 41 per cent, a wider margin than in any of the seven other European countries surveyed. In the US this view was even more pronounced – 77 per cent of respondents agreed with the proposition compared with just 20 per cent who disagreed.[30] This finding suggests that, while left-wing activists might view extreme inequality as 'unfair', a majority in Britain and America are likely to interpret economic differences resulting in unequal outcomes as a result of how hard people have worked, and thus see the unfairness in any attempt at redistribution or pre-distribution.

Similarly, comparative studies of attitudes to the super-rich have also found that people in the UK and US have generally more favourable attitudes towards rich people than are found elsewhere. In a survey covering Britain, the US, France, Germany, Spain, Italy and Sweden, respondents in Britain were the least likely to agree with statements that millionaires should be taxed more, that business leaders' pay should be reduced and that entrepreneurs who lost money as a result of risky business decisions deserved it, with Americans a close second.[31] Similarly, Brits were the least likely to blame the rich for problems in the world, and the most likely to pick positive terms from a list of words that could be used to describe the rich than negative ones. Again, Americans were the second most likely.

Intriguingly, while this endorses the idea of a free market 'Anglo-Saxon' worldview compared with continental Europe, where more social democratic attitudes generally prevail, this generalisation is subject to certain caveats. Respondents in Sweden had similar attitudes towards the rich to those in the UK and the US, significantly more positive than those in France, Germany, Italy or Spain. Whatever the extent of favourable attitudes to the rich, in each European country, including the UK, young people (under 30) viewed them more favourably than older people (over 60), whereas the reverse was true in the US.

The absence of an appetite for a major rebalancing of incomes and wealth is something that also emerges strongly from qualitative studies of public attitudes towards the super-rich. Focus groups convened by the Trust for London charitable foundation involved detailed discussions with a spectrum of Londoners about extreme levels of income and wealth and their effect on issues like social cohesion, democracy and social justice. But results showed there was no general support for the idea that there was a point at which levels of wealth become excessive or problematic.[32]

While the groups' views on the idea that the super-rich create prosperity and opportunity for others (the 'trickle-down effect') were mixed and there was recognition of the different ways in which people can get rich, including those who have inherited wealth or benefited from privileged connections ('silver spooners' as participants put it) or those who have just got lucky, there was also a strong conviction that many of those who have achieved extreme wealth have earned it through hard work and enterprise. Perhaps most importantly, there was a high level of resignation – the groups felt that the rich make the rules and there is very little that can be done about prevailing levels of inequality.

Research by the Tax Justice Network with voters in marginal constituencies across England and Wales produced similar findings.[33] Participants were alienated by language bashing the super-rich and generally felt that high levels of wealth result from hard work. Again, there was considerable cynicism and scepticism about the prospect of anything ever being done about the huge divides between the super-rich and everybody else.

By tackling the neglected problem of the super-rich we can improve society quite a lot

Unfortunately, the net result of this sentiment is that society is a lot worse-off than it would be if the total wealth and incomes generated by the UK and global economy were shared more evenly. By failing to contemplate more redistribution and pre-distribution from the super-rich we are ignoring an obvious and historically effective means of raising living standards that is completely compatible with (and would potentially enhance) greater aggregate economic growth.

This book intends to make a persuasive and optimistic case to that effect, arguing that tackling the super-rich should be the most urgent priority facing society. A major rebalancing of income and wealth is vitally necessary, entirely feasible and would lead to a major uplift in living standards for the overwhelming majority of people.

The problem of inequality is generally held to be more pronounced in anglophone economies – most obviously the US but also the UK and Australia and Canada – than other high-income countries, however it is an issue that countries across the world are facing to different degrees. This book will focus on the UK, but will also draw on evidence from other countries, particularly the US. It is intended to be of international relevance, given the shared problem of the super-rich and the common potential to improve society by achieving a more even distribution of income and wealth.

In the first chapter, the book discusses the concept of 'enough'. Any individual who achieves a level of income or wealth around the threshold for the top 1 per cent of the population of a high-income country can be considered very well rewarded for whatever successes they have achieved in life, with a very high level of material affluence. Redistributing or pre-distributing additional income or wealth beyond this point has no real downsides: those in the middle and the bottom benefit, while those at the top remain very well-off indeed.

The second chapter notes the extreme scale of concentrations of income and wealth and looks at the hypothetical increases in living standards that might be possible if current total income and wealth levels were more evenly distributed. Given the vast share of the totals that they hoard and the difference even a fraction of this would make to the wider population, it is extraordinary that releasing the fortunes captured by the super-rich is not considered one of the most urgent challenges of contemporary politics.

In chapter 3, the broader economic impacts of addressing the problem of the super-rich are discussed, including the growing body of evidence that suggests that tackling extreme concentrations of income and wealth would be good for aggregate economic growth, as well as ensuring a fairer distribution of existing resources.

Chapter 4 argues that the economic contribution of the super-rich has been wildly exaggerated. Their vast income and wealth levels are not necessary as a reward or incentive, and their ability and inclination to flee overseas to escape a slightly less servile policy regime is overstated, as is the extent to which we'd miss them if they went.

Chapter 5 then makes the complementary argument that a more evenly balanced distribution of income and wealth would also be a much more accurate reflection of how hard different people work and the contribution to society that they make. The outsized shares accruing to the super-rich are largely or completely undeserved, and we have a moral responsibility to reduce such extreme concentrations.

Finally, chapter 6 sets out some of the policies for tackling the problem of the super-rich. While this book focuses on *why* we need to tackle this problem, it is useful to note the proposals put forward by academics and researchers, and the policies that already exist in certain other countries, explaining *how* we might do so, demonstrating that it is an entirely realistic objective that could be rapidly begun.

The book concludes by noting the disastrous outcomes that our relaxed attitude to extreme concentrations of income and wealth has delivered, both in terms of inequality and living standards more generally. A major, transformative programme of redistribution and pre-distribution is a completely obvious, moderate and common-sense economic objective that ought to enjoy significant support from across the political spectrum as an uppermost priority for governments. We will not fulfil our potential to improve society without abolishing the super rich.

1
More than Enough

The essence of the problem of the super-rich is that their hoarding of such vast fortunes is needless and inefficient.

While some degree of inequality is arguably necessary to act as a reward or incentive for hard work or innovation, the levels of income and wealth that a small proportion of the population are accumulating go beyond, sometimes way beyond, what might reasonably be considered a valuable spur to productivity. It would surely be more sensible if some of these riches went to those who really need them, rather than enabling people who already have more than enough money and assets to be comfortable, contented and secure to pile up even more.

Extreme levels of income and wealth are not essential to happiness or financial security

Policymakers are strikingly incurious about this question of whether there might be such a thing as 'enough' but there is significant academic interest in the topic. Extensive research has been carried out on how much money one needs to achieve happiness and whether or not there comes a point at which increasing incomes or wealth stops delivering any increase in well-being. The debate is contested but the director of Oxford University's Wellbeing Research Centre suggested, in a *Guardian* interview in 2022, that increases beyond a disposable income of £100,000–£120,000 would no longer lead to any increase in positive emotions, and that most research shows that at some point there is a plateau where the relationship between increased income and increased happiness breaks down.[1]

The interview noted that there is general agreement on 'the flattening of the curve' meaning that the value of increases to income or wealth diminishes, as would be expected – a pay rise or other form of windfall is likely to bring about a smaller improvement to the happiness of someone raking in a six-figure salary, who already has a nice house, car and substantial savings, than it would for someone on the minimum wage or struggling with debt problems and unable to cover the cost of essentials like housing, clothing or food. This raises the question of whether money and assets accruing to people who are already extremely rich might be put to better use, in order to maximise aggregate well-being.

Some of the views expressed by the focus groups cited in the introductory chapter discussing attitudes towards the rich also suggest that really extreme incomes and wealth represent an excessive and unnecessary reward or incentive for business success. Many of the participants had a very vague definition of what it means to be 'rich' or 'wealthy'. Their comments depicted the rich as people they might know or whose lifestyles they might realistically emulate, and were framed in terms of consumption or lifestyle habits rather than particular levels of financial income or wealth. Examples of the degree of affluence participants in the Tax Justice Network groups had in mind included being sufficiently well-off to get a round of drinks in without worrying about money, or having something left over for a few 'luxuries' once all bills and essential living costs have been covered.[2]

It would be wrong to say that the groups saw this as the limit of what any person needs or should accumulate (indeed the focus groups convened by Trust for London definitively did not identify a 'riches line' above which they considered income or wealth levels to become problematic). But their interpretation of what it means to be rich implies first that, despite the ubiquity of TV shows like *Keeping Up with the Kardashians* and *Real Housewives of Beverley Hills*, or social media channels like the #richkidsofinstagram flaunting extraordinary wealth, many of the people responding negatively to policies or political rhetoric attacking the super-rich may not appreciate the scale of extreme income and wealth concentration. Second, it suggests that most people's aspirations are also a lot less greedy and acquisitive than those implied by the lifestyles of the super-rich.

This perception that a comfortable, affluent standard of living not far beyond that of a typical upper middle-class household in a high-income country is enough to qualify as 'rich' again prompts the question of whether people continuing to accumulate incomes and wealth over and above the amounts necessary to enable this lifestyle represents a reasonable, rational and efficient way to use the resources generated by our economy.

Reaching the 1 per cent is sufficient reward or incentive for success

Like the focus groups, this book does not seek to define a precise point at which someone becomes super-rich, nor does it advocate an absolute cap on income and wealth levels. But in high-income countries, the amounts sufficient to put the recipient in the richest 1 per cent of the population represent a useful 'ballpark' figure for the thresholds beyond which policymakers should be making much bolder and more concerted efforts to redistribute or pre-distribute income and wealth.

By definition the 1 per cent constitute a small number of people relative to society as a whole. There are some people who qualify for the top 1 per cent by income but not by wealth and vice versa, but as high incomes enable savings and investments leading to high wealth there is considerable overlap between the two groups. Similarly, the people that make up the 1 per cent may change from one year to the next as their income and wealth level changes, but anyone who gets there is likely to remain, relatively speaking, very rich. Income and wealth generally increase incrementally (think pay rises and promotions over the course of a career, or wealth building up through savings and investments). It is rare that people would experience a massive spike in income or wealth that would take them straight from the bottom or middle of the distribution to the top 1 per cent and then back again within the space of a year or two.

In the UK, the most recent data as of spring 2023 puts the threshold for the top 1 per cent of UK income taxpayers at £183,000 pre-tax and £121,000 post-tax.[3] For wealth (which is calculated on a household, rather than an individual basis), it would take almost £3.7 million to make the richest 1 per cent.[4]

The figures are even starker in the US, where the threshold for the richest 1 per cent of individuals by income is around $400,000 (pre-tax), while households need assets of over $11 million to qualify for the top 1 per cent by wealth.[5] The cost of living is also higher in America, but accounting for this still leaves the 1 per cent in the US much richer than their UK counterparts.

There are some caveats with these figures, and drawing a precise line for the top 1 per cent is a complicated exercise. The demarcation depends, for instance, on whether the calculations are pre- or post-tax, and whether they cover households, individuals or some other unit. As the 1 per cent are a small proportion of the population, with multiple sources of income and wealth, their riches are difficult to survey or measure. Expert estimates of what it takes to qualify for this group, or how much they hold in aggregate, may vary. But anyone who might plausibly be estimated to be around the top 1 per cent by income or wealth in the US or UK is very rich in any meaningful sense of the word, with a very high standard of living compared to the rest of the population of those countries, two of the richest in the world, never mind the population of the rest of the planet.

As has already been noted, some degree of inequality is perhaps inevitable and indeed may be reasonably defended as an incentive to reward hard work and innovation. But a level of material prosperity much greater than most people experience represents a sufficient reward or incentive, and income or wealth levels at the threshold of the top 1 per cent already satisfy this criterion.

The UK 1 per cent, with a pre-tax income of £183,000 or more, rake in at least seven times as much as the median UK income (that is, the taxpayer at the mid-point of the income distribution, richer than the poorest half of the population but poorer than the richest half) with a post-tax income of £24,600. The threshold for the top 1 per cent of the wealth distribution in the UK at £3.7 million is 12 times that of the median household wealth of £302,500. In America, an individual income on the threshold of the top 1 per cent of incomes is 8 times that at the median. In terms of wealth – which is calculated differently from the UK figures so comparisons are not straightforward – the top 1 per cent of households in the US are at least 91 times as rich as the median.[6]

Even compared with the modestly rich, those in the top 1 per cent are astonishingly well rewarded. In the UK, anyone qualifying for the top 1 per cent by income makes nearly four

times as much as those at the threshold for the top 10 per cent.
UK households in the wealthiest 1 per cent of the population
have, as a minimum, more than double the wealth required to
get into the top 10 per cent. As such, the prospect of increasing
income or wealth to levels sufficient to join the top 1 per cent
is still a major spur to work hard and be successful, even for
those who are already doing much better than 90 per cent of
the population.

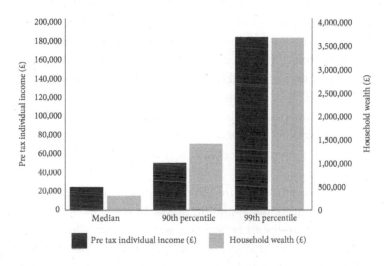

Figure 1   Incomes and wealth necessary to qualify for the richest
50 per cent, 10 per cent and 1 per cent of individuals (income) and
households (wealth) in the UK 2020–2021

Analysis of the kind of lifestyle that an income or wealth
level on the threshold of the top 1 per cent in the UK enables
emphasises why we should feel comfortable redistributing
or pre-distributing income and wealth over and above the
threshold.

Figures from the UK Office for National Statistics suggest
that a household in the top 10 per cent of the population

by disposable income (there is no breakdown for the top 1 per cent) spends, on average, about £66,000 a year.[7] This is roughly twice the amount spent by households in the sixth decile (i.e. those between the thresholds for the top 50 per cent and top 60 per cent, so with more to spend than over half the population).

The average size of the household in the sample is two people. Many individuals in the top 1 per cent might have a higher number of dependants – however, they might also have a partner bringing in additional income. While their increased income might mean higher living costs, even compared to the average across the top 10 per cent of households, these are sometimes limited by factors like time or physical capacity. For example, it is possible for richer people to shop at more expensive supermarkets or maintain a larger home, but there are physical limits to how much more they can eat and drink, or how many rooms they can occupy at a given time requiring heating and light.

Thus, the £66,000 figure provides a useful if rough guideline to the additional spending power of the 1 per cent. The difference from the £121,000 necessary to qualify for the top 1 per cent by post-tax income would still leave £55,000, which could cover private school fees for two children, a family holiday to the Maldives in a five-star resort and a deposit and monthly payments for a brand new top-of-the range Mercedes or BMW.[8] Remember, this is on top of the tens of thousands of pounds that the richest 10 per cent spend, on average, on housing, cars, savings and investments, clothes, electronic equipment and leisure activities, which is in turn more than twice as much those in the middle of the income distribution spend on these items.

These are only illustrative calculations, and of course the priorities of different households will vary. Some people might prefer saving for a rainy day over driving an ostentatious car. Anyone who doesn't feel that private education is necessary for their children could instead use the money to buy a one-hour guest appearance from James Corden at their birthday party or half a kilogram of cocaine.[9] But the overall picture is clear. A six-figure post-tax income in the UK enables the possibility of spending on luxury items far beyond the means of most ordinary people, and significantly higher spending on a home, car, holidays, clothes, appliances, recreation and lifestyle more generally.

The figures on wealth tell a similar story. The Office for National Statistics data suggests that household wealth of £3.6 million, on the threshold for the top 1 per cent, might encompass a pension pot of £1.7 million, £1 million worth of property, physical wealth (cars, art collection, fine china, etc.) worth £216,000 and the remaining £700,000 made up of financial wealth (for example, shares in companies or cash in the bank).[10]

Again, this is a really enormous level of wealth, far beyond the wildest dreams of the vast majority of people – and keep in mind that this is the *minimum* amount of wealth held by anyone in the 1 per cent. Many of those above the threshold have vastly more.

Clearly, anyone who reaches the top 1 per cent for income or wealth can be considered to have reached an extremely high standard of prosperity. Even if we accept the (deeply contentious) proposition that they have worked harder or contributed greater economic value than the wider population, they have been generously rewarded for that with a much higher level of material affluence. From the perspective of rewarding or incentivising hard work or innovation, thereby getting more of it across the economy, low six-figure incomes leading to the accumulation of wealth in the low millions ought to be enough. The notion that people would have no reason to work hard, start businesses, or invent useful products and services if incomes and wealth above these levels were redistributed or pre-distributed more substantially than is currently the case, is clearly preposterous.

Within the richest 1 per cent, incomes and wealth become increasingly gratuitous

The fact that beyond the threshold for the top 1 per cent, extraordinary levels of income and wealth exist, and that when we talk about tackling the problem of the super-rich, this is largely who we are talking about, is absolutely critical. It is not a case of going after the type of people described by the focus group participants as having achieved the level of modest affluence necessary to buy a round of drinks without worrying about the cost. Pre-distribution and redistribution efforts would not focus on taking the income and wealth of those at the threshold for the top 1 per cent in its entirety, but would target income and wealth *beyond* this threshold. This would mostly affect the fabulously rich, people who could easily afford to contribute more tax or increase the pay of the staff of the businesses they own and invest in, and still maintain a lifestyle way beyond the means of the wider population. Evidence from the aborted cut to the top rate of income tax in the UK in 2022 bears this point out – while the proposal would have seen the rate reduced on income above £150,000, two thirds of the benefit from the tax cut would have gone to those with an income of £500,000 or more because most of the income accruing to people making more than the £150,000 threshold goes to people bringing in way over this amount.[11]

Analysing the highest levels of income and wealth of those at the very top is notoriously difficult. The richer people are, the greater the likelihood that they can afford to employ skilled accountants and advisers to hide the details of their fortunes. Analysts compiling data rely heavily on survey responses and the smaller the subsection of the population they are trying to identify, the harder it becomes to get accurate and representative responses. So it is quite possible (many would say probable) that statistics on the incomes and wealth of those within the top 1 per cent and above may grossly understate how rich they are. However, official and unofficial statistics provide some insights into the fortunes of the very richest of the rich.

The threshold for the top 0.1 per cent by incomes (pre-tax) has been estimated at about £500,000, while there are around 2,500 income tax payers with pre-tax incomes of over £3.5 million.[12] High Pay Centre research on the pay of the CEOs of Britain's biggest companies, found that median CEO pay for the FTSE 100, the hundred biggest firms on the UK stock market, was £3.9 million in 2022. For the FTSE 250, the next biggest 250, it was £1.8 million. Altogether, FTSE 350 companies spent £1.3 billion on just 570 individual executives.[13]

The European Banking Authority (EBA) collects data on pay of high-earning bankers across the European Union, including the UK prior to Brexit. Their figures are collected and then published retrospectively so the most recent figures are from 2019. They show that there were over 3,500 bankers paid over €1 million in the UK that year (the EBA publishes its data in euros).[14] The total earnings of these individuals amounted to about €7.4 billion, or £6.5 billion.

In America, a larger and even more unequal economy, the figures are even more spectacular. The average annual earnings (covering income from employment but not other means, such as returns from investments) of the top 0.1 per cent of earners stood at over $3 million in 2021.[15] The median pay for a CEO of one of the 'S&P 500' group of the 500 largest stock exchange-listed American businesses was $14.5 million.[16]

Even making the generous assumption that they pay the full amount of tax, anyone in the UK top 0.1 per cent is still able to enjoy a lifestyle more than twice as luxurious as someone on the threshold of the top 1 per cent by post-tax income (and we have already described the opulence one can enjoy upon reaching the richest 1 per cent). Once someone reaches this level of income you begin to wonder where it might all go, bearing in mind that one can only wear so many designer clothes at once or eat so much caviar per day.

For the CEOs and bankers with annual pay of over £1 million, it really is the case that, even with lavish spending habits, they can support an opulent lifestyle of fast cars, fine wines and glamorous holidays and still have plenty left over to give their kids a very generous head start in life, provided they invest it in a vaguely sensible way.

Billionaire wealth is on another level still. The 2023 edition of the Sunday Times Rich List found that Britain is now home to 171 billionaires, with the wealth of the 350 households on the rich list of the richest families in Britain ranging from £350 million, up to a stupendous £30 billion.[17] Across the Atlantic, the ten richest Americans alone have a combined net worth of over $1 trillion![18] There are 735 American billionaires in total, with a combined wealth of $4.5 trillion.

The words 'super-rich' or 'wealthy' are almost inadequate to describe such extreme concentrations of wealth, and it is a struggle to find analogies that can convey them either. If someone's ancestors had made £1,000 a day every day for the nearly 21 centuries that have passed since Julius Caesar landed in Britain and this accumulated to them in its entirety in 2023, they still wouldn't be a billionaire (they'd be almost

£250 million short and something like 229th on the list of the richest Britons).

Assuming jackpots of £2 million on Wednesday nights and £3.8 million on Saturdays, it would take 346 consecutive UK lottery wins to achieve billionaire status, picking the correct numbers twice a week at odds of about 45 million to 1 each time, for every draw for nearly three and a half years.[19]

Any individual billionaire could, as of spring 2023, purchase every property listed on Rightmove in the SW1 postcode (considered to be the most desirable part of London) with a value of over £20 million, and still have about £500 million left over.[20]

That would be more than enough for at least a couple of superyachts, such as the 73-metre *Axioma*, which contains a swimming pool, a 3D cinema room, a gym, a Jacuzzi and a fully equipped spa, previously owned by a Russian oligarch until it was confiscated by the authorities in Gibraltar and sold for £35 million.[21] Some of the remaining £65 million could go on a few helicopters, at an average cost of $2 million according to industry data.[22]

The super-rich are at best a necessary evil

If asked to describe the ideal balance of resources, no sensible person would suggest a scenario where millions of people live in crippling, agonising poverty – or even just struggle a bit to cover their bills and essentials – while a handful of super-rich individuals can afford more superyachts, mansions and helicopters than they could ever feasibly use. Lifestyles and consumption above the 1 per cent thresholds increasingly go so far beyond what could be considered a sensible reward for innovation and productivity that no-one could argue that existing distributions of income and wealth represent an optimal outcome. It is totally legitimate to think that efforts to redistribute or pre-distribute more of the vast fortunes currently accruing to the super-rich would inadvertently do more economic harm than good. But reasonable people should surely at least start from the point that, even if these arguments are correct, such extreme income and wealth accumulation is at absolute best a necessary evil.

This book will hopefully persuade readers that it is not that necessary, and that while, on an individual level, super-rich people may not literally be evil (at least, not in all cases), the avoidable hardship that results from extreme concentrations of income and wealth might fairly be described as such. The next chapter, showing the immense difference that the excess incomes and wealth of the super-rich could make to wider living standards if they were shared more evenly, will illustrate this point.

2
The Opportunity Cost
of the Super-Rich

The previous chapter highlights the inefficiency of extreme concentrations of income and wealth. The super-rich have more than they need to reward and incentivise innovation and productivity. But to understand how much this inefficiency matters from a practical perspective, it is important to examine what the scale of excessive incomes and wealth beyond the top 1 per cent thresholds represents in terms of the potential 'opportunity cost' of the super-rich. National economies generate vast incomes and wealth for this tiny proportion of the population. What kind of difference would it make if their money and assets were distributed more widely and evenly across society?

Income and wealth accumulation is not necessarily a 'zero-sum game', whereby any amount taken from those at the top automatically becomes available to those in the middle or at the bottom. But this chapter will show that the fortunes of the super-rich are theoretically huge enough to fund dramatic improvements to living standards and still leave enough left over to represent a considerable incentive or reward for success. Therefore policymakers should at least be thinking more seriously about mechanisms to re-distribute or pre-distribute this immense repository of excess income and wealth.

The 1 per cent hold a vast share of income and wealth

As we have already noted, estimating the precise levels and shares of the income and wealth of the super-rich is challenging. However, research consistently implies broadly similar conclusions regarding the potential to raise living standards through a more even division of resources.

A 2020 study by the CAGE Research Centre at Warwick University found that the richest 1 per cent of the UK population captured around 17 per cent of total pre-tax UK incomes in 2018 (the most recent year for which data was available at the time).[1] This effectively means that of every £100 going into people's pockets in Britain that year, £17 went to the top 1 per cent.

The study found that over the previous 20 years, save for a drop-off in the aftermath of the financial crisis, the richest 1 per cent had steadily increased their share of total incomes from just under 14 per cent in 1997. In the context of total national incomes, amounting to over a trillion pounds, the three per centage point difference between 14 per cent and 17 per cent equates to tens of billions going to the richest 1 per cent of the UK population rather than the other 99 per cent.

The World Inequality Database (WID), a resource maintained by academic economists comparing international income and wealth distributions, puts their most recent confirmed figure for the share of total pre-tax incomes captured by the richest 1 per cent in the UK at 13 per cent, in 2018 (the Warwick University study implies the WID figures underestimate the top 1%'s income from capital gains, hence the different figures).[2] This is almost double the lowest point recorded by the WID over its 200 year analysis, in 1980 and 1981, and is higher than any point in the half century following the second world war as the share of incomes captured by the 1 per cent declined over the post-war period before steadily increasing throughout the 1980s and 1990s.

The WID suggests the top 1 per cent in France and Germany capture a similar share of total incomes to the UK but in many other European countries they take significantly less – for example the most recent confirmed figures for the Netherlands, Belgium and Sweden show the richest 1 per cent in those countries taking a share of around 9 per cent of the total. However, the share of total incomes accruing to the super-rich is much higher in the US, where the top 1 per cent take 19 per cent of total incomes, almost one dollar in every five made by Americans!

It is a similar story with wealth inequality. The CAGE Centre at Warwick University estimated in 2021 that the richest 1 per cent of families in the UK controlled about 23 per cent of total wealth.[3] Again, this reflects a similar historic trend to income inequality in the UK, with the share captured by the 1 per cent falling throughout the twentieth century, to the 15–20 per cent range in the late 1970s and early 1980s and then rising steadily from there.

Internationally, the UK seems less of an outlier in terms of wealth inequality. The WID records the share of total UK wealth captured by the richest 1 per cent as hovering at around 21 per cent since 2016 – compared to less than 5 per cent held by the bottom 50 per cent.[4] The share going to the top 1 per cent in the UK is lower than the WID figures for France (26 per cent), Germany (27 per cent) or the USA (35 per cent) but still significantly higher than Belgium (15 per cent) or the Netherlands (16 per cent).

The UBS *Global Wealth Report* comparing household wealth across different countries produces similar findings to the WID, based on calculations using the Gini coefficient, a technical measure of inequality that focuses on general divisions in society, rather than just the top 1 per cent versus everybody else. Using this measure, UBS estimates that the UK has greater wealth inequality than Australia, Japan, Italy and Belgium, about the same as France, and less than Sweden, Denmark, Germany, Austria, Switzerland, the Netherlands, Canada and the US.[5] However, their report notes that entitlements to generous social security arrangements common in European countries, including state pensions that provide a much higher proportion of income in retirement than in the UK, are not counted towards wealth levels. Similarly, in countries with higher levels (and standards) of social housing and more extensive long-term protections for renters, there is less pressure to own property and thus property ownership is more concentrated among the rich. It should also be emphasised that because wealth is taxed (and therefore recorded) less extensively or systematically than income, and is affected by factors like changing asset values, it can be more difficult to measure. So international comparisons of wealth inequality have certain limitations and might be less reflective of relative inequality of living standards than comparisons of income inequality levels.

Overall though, the picture is pretty clear. The proportion of total incomes captured by the super-rich in the UK is higher than at almost any time since the second world war. It is higher than in many other comparable countries. The richest 1 per cent of the UK population by wealth are not such outliers internationally, but their share of total wealth is extraordinary on its own terms. It is much greater than the proportion of incomes captured by the top 1 per cent, representing over a fifth and approaching a quarter of total UK wealth. This share also appears to be gradually increasing.

In the US, the richest 1 per cent enjoy a greater share of both total income and wealth than in any other major economy and this has been steadily and significantly increasing for the past 40 years. In other parts of Western Europe, increases have been less constant or dramatic but again the share of both income and wealth captured by the top 1 per cent has grown over the past 40 years.

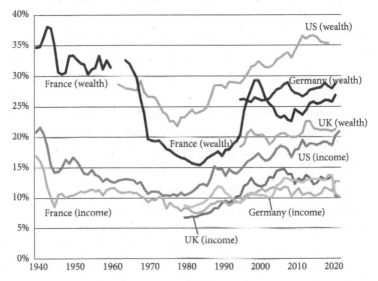

Figure 2 Share of income and wealth accruing to the richest 1 per cent in the UK, USA, France and Germany

Existing income and wealth shared more evenly would mean far higher living standards

While the top 1 per cent represent a very small proportion of the total population, there are enough of them, and they are all rich enough, to mean that the sum of their aggregate fortunes is quite massive. In the UK, 1 per cent of the adult population amounts to almost 600,000 people or nearly 300,000 households. Given that the levels of income and wealth needed just to qualify for the top 1 per cent are substantial and their shares of total income and wealth are so large, the combined value of that income and wealth is enormous.

If a greater proportion of these riches instead accrued to the other 99 per cent of the population, this would have a transformative effect on living standards for the majority. The current distribution, whereby an enormous share of incomes and wealth flow to a tiny number of people, is profoundly inefficient. It isn't just that those beyond the top 1 per cent threshold are a lot richer than everybody else. It's that the total value of the excess incomes and wealth that they capture is enough to make an enormous difference to wider society if it was distributed more evenly. Existing resources shared more sensibly would mean much more widespread prosperity. The incomes and wealth of the super-rich represent a gigantic fund that could be used to make the world better in all manner of different ways, rather than just making rich people even richer

Simple mathematical exercises examining potential ways to divide up total incomes and wealth demonstrate this point. The CAGE analysis of UK income distribution implies around £220 billion in total incomes accruing to the richest 1 per cent (which equates to an average of roughly £400,000 annual income for each person in the 1 per cent).[6] In a hypothetical scenario where the total incomes in the UK remained at around the level implied by the CAGE study, but the share captured by the richest 1 per cent was reduced by 10 percentage points from 17 per cent to 'only' 7 per cent, with the difference being shared with the remaining 99 per cent of the adult population, average incomes for the top 1 per cent would remain around £160,000. Meanwhile, the difference would be worth close to £2,500 more for every adult in the 99 per cent.

The High Pay Centre and the Autonomy think tank carried out a similar analysis in 2020, focused on income from earnings only, intended to identify the potential of a 'maximum wage'. The study examined the impact a limit on the pay of top earners might have, if all earnings beyond that limit were instead redistributed to those in the middle and at the bottom. It found that if the cap were set at £187,000, moving any income above this amount to the pay of the 3 million lowest earning full-time workers in Britain would raise their minimum annual pay to over £20,000.[7] Only 0.6 per cent of earners (the proportion earning over £187,000 a year) would need to see their earnings reduced in order to fund this re-balancing, which would eliminate poverty pay at a stroke.

To some extent, these kinds of exercises already happen through taxation and redistribution – the CAGE study notes that post-tax the income share of the top 1 per cent falls to 12.3 per cent. But there is important context to this. Firstly, 12.3 per cent represents a very large share of total incomes held by the super-rich even after taxation, meaning that there is still considerable scope to raise living standards through additional re-balancing of the distribution in favour of the 99 per cent. Further reducing the share of the 1 per cent would mean billions more for the wider population. Secondly, pre-tax inequality is also important. The huge share captured by the richest 1 per cent highlights the potential to raise incomes by ensuring a more even balance of the pay and profits generated by large employers, before resorting to taxation. While we need higher and more progressive taxes on the super-rich, measures that prevent them from accumulating such a disproportionate share of income in the first place are likely to be more sustainable and empowering, as later chapters will discuss.

Hypothetical exercises for rebalancing incomes in the US suggest even more spectacular potential to raise living standards through redistribution and pre-distribution.[8] If the total incomes accruing to the top 1 per cent as estimated by the WID were merely halved, and the difference shared across the wider population, it would be worth close to $6,000 for every adult in America. This would still leave the 1 per cent in the US with a greater share of total incomes than the WID has recorded in recent years for the richest 1 per cent in European countries such as France, Belgium or Norway.

As wealth is distributed more unevenly than income, the scope to achieve major benefits for society through the pre-distribution or redistribution of wealth is even greater.

The estimate of a 23 per cent share of total wealth held by the wealthiest 1 per cent of UK families equates to an astonishing £3.5 trillion in wealth held by this small proportion of the population.[9] To give a visual illustration, it would require about £1.7 trillion in cash to cover the entire floorspace of every home in Great Britain with £5 notes (a shade under £60,000 – on average – per home). Subtracting £1.7 trillion from the £3.5 trillion wealth of the richest 1 per cent would still leave them with £1.8 trillion. This £1.8 trillion would mean that even after £2 trillion of their wealth was reallocated, every super-rich family of the 1 per cent would still have an average fortune of around £2.6 million per adult per family (plus their carpet of fivers).[10]

This is not to suggest that people should start writing to their MPs demanding a 'cash carpet' funded by the 1 per cent. Obviously much of their wealth represents the paper value of assets like shares or property, rather than money in the bank. There are only about £80 billion worth of bank notes in circulation, barely 5 per cent of the amount needed to cover every home, so the practicalities would be challenging, to say the least. It would also be quite regressive as richer people tend to have bigger houses with more floorspace so they would benefit from bigger pay-outs.

However, the imaginary carpet-fitting exercise does hammer home the point that the super-rich are not just rich compared to everybody else. They are rich enough to dole out tens of thousands of pounds worth of assets to every household in the country, a life-changing amount of wealth, while retaining multi-million-pound fortunes themselves.

And if you argue that a rebalancing on this scale is unfeasible or undesirable; that average wealth of £2.6 million for every adult in every family in the top 1 per cent is not enough; and that they deserve way more than £1.8 trillion between them – smaller scale transfers would still have a major impact. Just 1 per cent of the wealth of the top 1 per cent – £35 billion – would be about the amount required to make all bus travel free for low-income households and end homelessness, while still leaving enough left over to cover the annual running costs of the Foreign, Commonwealth and Development Office.[11]

Even when focusing solely on the most incomprehensibly wealthy families within the top 1 per cent, the potential to achieve positive change through wealth redistribution or pre-distribution is enormous. The £800 billion that constitutes the total wealth of the entrants on the Sunday Times Rich List is greater than the *Global Wealth Report*'s estimates for the total wealth of the populations of entire countries, including some very large – though admittedly low-income – states like Pakistan and Nigeria (both countries of over 200 million people), as well as smaller but middle-income Ukraine (44 million people) Romania (20 million) or more prosperous Finland (6 million).[12] A few hundred American billionaires with $4.5 trillion collective wealth hold more than all the household wealth reported for large middle-income countries like Russia (143 million people) and Indonesia (274 million), as well as medium sized rich ones like Saudi Arabia (36 million) and Sweden (10 million). Again, this raises the issue of rewards and incentives. No doubt some of these billionaires have had business success for which they deserve to be recognised. But have they really contributed more to humanity than every person in Nigeria or Sweden combined? Might the prospect of riches equivalent to the entire population of a small town, or even a village, as opposed to an entire country, not have been enough to incentivise their efforts?

Transferring the assets of the 350 UK rich list entrants, involving all their financial wealth plus absolutely everything they own, anywhere, to the population of Finland would probably be excessive, not to mention difficult to coordinate. But again, even a fraction of billionaire wealth would be totally transformative if distributed more efficiently. The charity Action against Hunger suggest that 783 million people are undernourished, while over 2.3 billion people lack access to basic sanitation facilities or latrines according to Oxfam.[13] The head of the UN's World Food Programme has said that it would cost $40 billion a year to end world hunger by 2030. Between 2021 and 2022, $40 billion was roughly the increase in the wealth of the top 250 entrants on the UK rich list – that is, 250 households in the UK alone held enough wealth to cover the cost of ensuring that no-one in the world went hungry in 2022, without even touching the record-breaking billionaire or multi-millionaire fortunes they enjoyed in 2021. This gives an idea of the magnitude of what global billionaire wealth could achieve if it was used for humanitarian purposes, rather than being held by a handful of people who would remain far richer than 99 per cent of the population, with even 1 per cent of their current wealth.

Even within individual employers, there is massive potential for fairer division of pay and profits

The potential of redistribution or pre-distribution is also borne out by looking specifically at how it might apply on an employer-by-employer basis, rather than across the economy as a whole. Large companies are extraordinary generators of wealth and income for the super-rich so if it were possible to distribute this more evenly, the impact on wider living standards would be significant.

UK banks publish quite detailed data about the pay across their workforce, from the superstar investment bankers to branch staff around the country, and thus provide an enlightening case study of the potential impact of rebalancing the pay of top earners and everybody else. A 2020 High Pay Centre study of the UK's biggest banks (Barclays, HSBC, Lloyds, NatWest and Standard Chartered) calculated the impact of redistributing 50 per cent of the pay of the top earners at the bank (around 1 per cent of their total employees) to the lowest earning half of the banks' employee population. The research found that this redistribution would enable a pay rise of between £2,000 and £16,000 (depending on the company) for over 200,000 lower-earning employees. Pay for the 3,000 top earners across these four banks would still average between £218,000 and £452,000 across the different banks.[14]

Table 1   Potential to redistribute pay of high earners at UK banks

Company	Total employees	High earners in key risk-taking roles	Spend on high earners (m)	Potential redistribution per below median employee (50 per cent of high earnings)	Average high earner pay post-redistribution
Barclays	90,441	1,590	£1,401	£15,490	£441k
HSBC	242,850	1,212	$1440	$5,930	$594k
Lloyds	72,626	280	£191.20	£2,632	£341k
RBS	67,600	588	£311.20	£4,604	£265k
Standard Chartered	86,268	630	$613	$7,105	$487k

Banks are unusual in terms of their number of very high-earning employees and the detailed regulations that they must comply with. Therefore, whether this kind of rebalancing is even hypothetically possible in other industries is harder to prove. But High Pay Centre data suggests that more than one in five FTSE 350 companies pay their CEOs at least 100 times their median UK employee, and at over one in ten companies, at least a quarter of the workforce are paid less than £20,000.[15] These figures don't include outsourced workers, who tend to be lower paid, so it is likely that they probably understate the true extent of the imbalance.

Just half of the £1.3 billion that the High Pay Centre found was paid to FTSE 350 executives in 2022 would fund a £3,000 pay rise for over 200,000 workers.[16] Alternatively, it could be ploughed back into training, production or research and development, giving a huge boost to the UK's growth and productivity. And the executive pay figures typically only cover the two highest-earning executives at the companies, without including other senior managers who are also paid in the hundreds of thousands or even millions. So there are good grounds to think that large UK employers could significantly raise productive investment or pay for a very large number of workers by reducing their expenditure on a relatively small number of high earners.

This is also the case in the US, where a 2022 study by the AFL-CIO trade union group found that median CEO to median employee pay ratio in the S&P 500 is 354:1.[17] The median pay for a CEO of these companies was $14.5 million. In 63 of the companies the CEO was paid over $50 million.[18] Again, it's worth spelling out the alternative ways to spend this kind of money. Anyone paid $50 million could afford to give away 90 per cent of their pay, use it to fund a $5,000 dollar pay rise for 20,000 low-earning colleagues, and still claim a lottery win-sized annual pay award of $5 million.

And pay is just one element of the riches generated from corporate revenues. The FTSE 100 companies have a combined value of around £2 trillion.[19] Research from the High Pay Centre, the Commonwealth think tank and the Trades Union Congress found that the FTSE 100 companies as constituted in 2019 (i.e. prior to the Covid pandemic) had generated £551 billion in profits, paying out £442 billion to their shareholders over the previous five years.[20]

Share ownership and corporate profits overwhelmingly and increasingly accrue to those at the top. Shareholdings are one of the least equal forms of wealth ownership, with the richest 1 per cent of the UK population by income holding greater share-based wealth than the poorest 90 per cent.[21] While pension-based wealth (including shareholdings via a pension fund) is more evenly distributed, it is still highly unequal, with the richest 20 per cent of UK households holding nearly half of all pensions wealth.[22] Of low-paid full-time workers in the private sector, paid less than £200 a week, 41 per cent do not belong to a pension scheme.[23] Furthermore, the proportion of corporate profits that reach UK pension savers – rich or poor – has declined dramatically, with pension fund ownership of UK companies falling from around a third of shareholdings in 1990 to about 6 per cent.[24] This represents a major change in the link between the fortunes of corporate Britain and the wider prosperity of society. It means that economic policies that maximise the ability of corporations to generate vast profits in the hope that these profits somehow trickle down to the wider population are likely to be far less effective.

Conversely, redirecting even a small proportion of profits and returns to shareholders to the wider population would make a major difference to people's quality of life, while still enabling the companies to sustain healthy profits. With FTSE100 companies employing 5 million employees world-wide, just 10 per cent of the shareholder returns identified by the High Pay Centre research would have equated to around £9,000 more per worker over five years.

The data in the US paints a similar picture, with much larger companies and much larger disparities. The richest 1 per cent of Americans own 38 per cent of all shareholdings, including investments through pension funds and other forms of indirect ownership – the poorest 90 per cent of Americans own 16 per cent, and the poorest 50 per cent just 7 per cent.[25] According to calculations by researchers at Harvard University, making all US companies 30 per cent employee-owned (i.e. effectively transferring shares to workers at the compa-nies) would increase the average wealth of the least wealthy 75 per cent of Americans by over $90,000, while reducing the wealth share of the richest 1 per cent to 29 per cent of all wealth, a figure that would still be higher than in most other high-income economies, and higher than the share in the US itself as recently as 1995.[26]

Misguided fear of economic risks concentrates income and wealth inefficiently

It is important to recognise that the calculations in this chapter are hypothetical. We cannot just alter the balance of income and wealth distributions with a click of the fingers. There is not a fixed pool of aggregate income or wealth for each country that can be periodically divided up based on what society thinks is a fair level of inequality. The kind of policies that would lead to a different balance between the super-rich and everybody else would also lead to different outcomes in terms of total incomes and wealth.

Individual companies do effectively allocate their pay-outs to investors, executives and the wider workforce by dividing up the budget they set and the revenues they generate, so estimates of how these might theoretically be rebalanced are less abstract than those based on total incomes and wealth across the economy as a whole. But again, the policies that would lead to workers gaining at the expense of executives and investors might also affect companies' revenues, so the calculations just give an idea of the theoretical potential of redistributing or pre-distributing away from the super-rich rather than precise sums that would be reallocated.

However, it should also be emphasised that there are many reasons, discussed in subsequent chapters, to think that more equal distributions and the policies intended to achieve them would lead to the aggregate levels of income and wealth generated by both entire economies and individual businesses being *higher* rather than *lower* than is currently the case. The fact that prosperous countries like Norway or the Netherlands have achieved both higher overall prosperity and much lower inequality suggests that it should be possible to achieve this in other countries too. Therefore, the illustrative calculations in this chapter may actually understate the benefits of rebalancing incomes and wealth to the majority of the population.

What is indisputable is that the super-rich have sufficient income and wealth to enable a major uplift in living standards if this was shared more evenly, without really compromising their immense prosperity. It then becomes a matter of whether their huge fortunes represent a fair, proportionate and economically sensible outcome, and, if not, whether there are policies to address it and how they might effectively be applied. Given the sheer scale of the income and wealth held by the super-rich, and the theoretically possible enormous positive changes that could be brought about if their riches were distributed more evenly and efficiently, it is really sur-prising that policymakers are not more interested in these questions.

This in part reflects the unthinking assumption that attempts to do anything bolder to address the problem of the super-rich would cause wider economic harm. The association of redistributive or pre-distributive policy measures with lower aggregate levels of income and wealth is deeply entrenched.

But this chapter has hopefully provided some idea of the size of the gains that society might stand to make from tackling the problem of the super-rich. And the next chapter will discuss why politicians' fear of doing so is completely misplaced.

3
The Economic Case for Equality

There are some people who argue that action to rebalance the extreme concentrations of incomes and wealth discussed in the previous chapter would disincentivise or inhibit creativity, innovation and business growth to the extent that everybody's living standard would suffer.

If they were right, this could be grounds for tolerating the existence of the super-rich. We would just have to sit back, watch their yachts getting bigger and their pet projects more ludicrous (US billionaires Jeff Bezos and Elon Musk are obsessed with space travel while German American billionaire Peter Thiel is keen to build human settlements at sea) and hope that we can 'grow the pie' so much that even the crumbs of it accruing to those in the middle and at the bottom get big enough to support a decent standard of living.

If that sounds utterly bleak, we needn't worry because fortunately it isn't necessary at all. Instead, we can be increasingly confident that a massive, ambitious programme of pre-distribution and redistribution would deliver economic growth while also ensuring its proceeds are more evenly shared, resulting in the biggest possible improvements in living standards for the widest number of people.

This view may not be held by enough mainstream politicians, but it is supported by a growing number of credible economic voices. The Nobel Prize-winning economist Joseph Stiglitz has suggested a top rate of income tax of 70 per cent on the highest earners.[1] The International Monetary Fund

(IMF) have said that wealth taxes could be an effective way of restoring public services in the aftermath of the Covid-19 pandemic.[2] Sometimes these arguments have even be made by the super-rich themselves. The Patriotic Millionaires group active in the US and UK say that there is no economic or moral basis for the extreme riches that they and their peers have accrued, and campaign for measures to achieve a more even distribution.[3]

How income and wealth are distributed determines our prosperity

The first and most obvious piece of 'real-world' evidence supporting the arguments made by Stiglitz, the IMF and the Patriotic Millionaires, and rebutting the claim that the super-rich are an economic necessity, comes from the fact that different countries already adopt different levels of tolerance for extreme concentrations of income and wealth. Those that are more assertive in terms of redistribution and pre-distribution tend to deliver higher standards of living for a broader range of people than those that aren't.

Data on household incomes across different countries compiled by the *Financial Times* in 2022 neatly illustrates this point. According to the analysis, disposable household income at the 97th percentile of the national income distribution (i.e. the threshold for the top 3 per cent) in the UK in 2019 (the most recent year for which data from all countries is shown) was higher than in most of the north-west European countries with which we compare ourselves economically, including France, Germany, Belgium, the Netherlands, Denmark and Sweden.[4] However, median incomes in those countries were higher than in the UK by a range of between 3 per cent and 23 per cent. Households at the fifth percentile (the threshold for the poorest 5 per cent of households) had incomes between 10 per cent and 49 per cent higher than those at the same position in the UK income distribution.

The uneven balance of incomes means that while the richest people in the UK are usually richer than the richest people in most north-west European countries, the majority of the population are poorer than the majority in those countries. Indeed, many people in countries commonly considered to be a lot poorer than the UK are also often doing much better than their UK counterparts. The *Financial Times* data suggests that the poorest 5 per cent households in the UK are poorer than the poorest 5 per cent in Czechia and Slovenia, former Eastern bloc countries that only emerged from totalitarian communist dictatorships in the 1990s. By contrast, at the 97th percentile, income for the richest UK households is over 50 per cent higher than for the richest Slovenians and Czechs.

Most of the north-western European countries discussed (except France, which is broadly equal to the UK) have higher

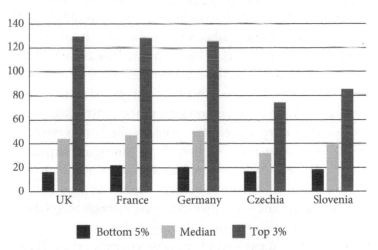

Figure 3   Household income at the 5th, median and 97th percentile point, 2019 ($000s, constant 2019 PPPs)

GDP per capita than the UK, implying that there is more to go round for everybody. However, the fact that the UK's lowest- and middle-income households lag behind their counterparts in other parts of Western Europe, while the UK's rich are generally richer than the richest in these other countries, highlights the fact that uneven distribution of income makes things worse for those with low and middle incomes in the UK than would be the case if we had an income distribution more similar to that of our neighbours. The fact that most of those countries are also richer than Britain demonstrates that we need not fear the economic impact of efforts to equalise incomes.

Part of the reason that the income distribution in these other Western European countries is more even is because pre-distribution and redistribution at the expense of the super-rich are more central to their economic model. Almost all of these countries levy a higher top rate of personal income tax than the UK.[5] They mostly have a higher rate of corporation tax, meaning a bigger share of big companies' profits goes to public services for all, rather than to pay-outs to disproportionately wealth investors.[6] They all have either a much higher proportion of workers who are members of trade unions or are covered by collective bargaining agreements where their pay is agreed as part of a negotiating process involving unions and workforce representatives.[7] These collective agreements mean that lower-paid workers have stronger bargaining power relative to high earners than when they negotiate their pay individually. They are also able to capture a bigger share of the revenue generated for their company through their labour that might otherwise go to wealthy investors.

Essentially, ordinary people in these countries typically are better off than in the UK because their governments have a less servile attitude towards the super-rich. It will be difficult to raise living standards in Britain without understanding this and replicating it. Far from being a risk to the UK economy, taking on the super-rich is an economic necessity. Countries where poor people are poorer than the poorest in the Czech Republic or Slovenia cannot afford to have rich people who are richer than the richest Dutch or Germans.

The case for tackling the problem of the super-rich in the USA is less clear based on the *Financial Times* data. Though it is one of the most unequal high-income countries, the analysis suggests that it is not only rich Americans but also those at the median income level for the country that have higher incomes than their international equivalents. However, even in America those at the 10th percentile point, representing the cut-off point for the poorest 10 per cent of households (the analysis did not include data on the poorest 5 per cent), were poorer than their counterparts in Slovenia. Incomes at the 10th percentile in the north-west European countries previously cited were between 4 per cent and 38 per cent higher than in the US. If raising the incomes of the poorest in society is deemed to be a priority, this is still very strong evidence that America should focus much more on redistributing and pre-distributing away from the super-rich. Furthermore, there are very many reasons why America's economy might deliver higher incomes at the top and middle of the distribution than Western Europe – for example, its size and natural resource wealth, and an economy that is culturally and regulatorily homogeneous. Americans and their money can move around the US much more easily than people can work or make investments across borders in Europe, given the different languages and business traditions. Crucially, Americans also work significantly longer hours than Europeans, which helps to make some of them materially richer but at the expense of leisure time and quality of life.[8] It is therefore very unlikely that median incomes in the US are higher by international standards because the country takes a more supine approach towards the super-rich, whereas low incomes in America probably are lower for that reason.

Redistribution and pre-distribution would support growth and stability

Of course, it would be wrong to say that all other countries have to do to solve the problem of the super-rich is to copy the policy solutions in north-west Europe. While the issues with income inequality may be less extreme than in Britain or the US, European countries also suffer from the problem of the super-rich to differing extents, and have scope to raise living standards for the majority by achieving a more even distribution.

Therefore, it is important to emphasise that the evidence highlighting the malign economic impact of the super-rich goes well beyond these international comparisons. There is a substantial body of research suggesting that bolder action to address concentrations of income and wealth could make economies stronger and more resilient, rather than creating economic risks.

For example, there is growing interest in the extent to which the super-rich are a source of economic instability. A 2021 paper by US economists illustrates how the extreme wealth of those at the top leads to increased debt levels for ordinary households, resulting in wider economic instability and poorer conditions for growth and prosperity.

The paper suggests that the increasing wealth of the richest 1 per cent in the US was associated with 'dis-saving' by the poorest 90 per cent of the population.[9] The increase in savings by the wealthiest 1 per cent of Americans since the 1980s has risen in a similar proportion to the increase in levels of household (and government) debt. Around 30 per cent of the increase in household debt of the poorest 90 per cent was ultimately financed by the wealthiest 1 per cent. As the wealthiest become richer, their 'savings glut' was lent to the poor to compensate for the missing wealth that would accumulate to them if the balance of wealth distribution were maintained or made more even.

Heightened debt brings about considerable stress in the households affected, and potentially long-term financial problems, plus wider economic instability when this is repeated on a national or international scale. Indebted households are also much less likely to undertake the entrepreneurial or creative/artistic pursuits on which prosperity and so much else depend, simply because servicing their debt becomes such an overriding priority.

While the increase in the wealth share of the 1 per cent in the UK has been less spectacular than in the US, it has slowly increased in recent years, and is much greater than the income share of the top 1 per cent. It is intuitive that extreme concentrations of wealth and income might lead to instability – if huge gaps in income and wealth create wider differences in living standards, then the pressure on households at the bottom and in the middle to take on greater and riskier levels of debt to keep up with those pulling away from them increases. When much of this debt is ultimately owed to those at the top, the destabilising effect become self-perpetuating.

This suggests that stopping such excess wealth accruing to the super-rich and redirecting it to the wider population could reduce economic instability.

Similarly, it is widely agreed that richer people have a lower 'marginal propensity to consume'. This essentially means that people who have less money are more likely to spend any additional amount that they receive than people who have more money. Again, this is intuitive. People who can't afford to eat as much as they need are definitely likely to spend any additional income on food, creating prosperity for the businesses that produce, transport and sell food and the people that work in them. People who already have as much food (or clothes or cars or holidays) as their time and digestive capacity can process are more likely to stash any extra away.

Research by the Federal Reserve Bank of Boston estimated that households in the bottom fifth of the wealth distribution in the US are roughly ten times as likely to spend additional income than those in the top fifth. The same research estimated that if the $1.1 trillion value of the 13.5 percentage point increase in the income share of the top 1 per cent in the US between 1979 and 2007 were transferred to the other 99 per cent, this would generate an additional $230 billion of annual consumer spending in the US.[10]

It follows that either redistributive or pre-distributive measures directing money that would otherwise go to the super-rich to the wider population would lead to higher aggregate spending, helping to stimulate the economy – a further reason to encourage policies that might lead to a more even balance of income and wealth.

The super-rich exacerbate the climate, housing and social crises

Beyond the fact that it is generally economically destabilising and inefficient, the hoarding of extreme incomes and wealth by the super-rich also contributes to certain specific outcomes that are really bad for the rest of society, and further strengthens the socio-economic case for redistribution and pre-distribution.

First, the risk of dangerous climate change is greatly exacerbated by the super-rich and their super-sized greenhouse gas emissions. Chapter 1 looked at opulent lifestyles, noting the incredible levels of consumption enabled by income and wealth above the top 1 per cent threshold. This has significant environmental consequences. Bloomberg estimate that a four-hour flight on a private jet emits as much carbon as the average European Union citizen emits in a year.[11] A study of the carbon footprints of 20 well-known billionaires found that the annual emissions associated with their homes and modes of transport (principally superyachts and private jets) amounted to about 160,000 tonnes of CO_2, an average of 8,190 tonnes each.[12]

For an equivalent figure for the UK population as a whole, the average carbon emissions per person from transport and heating and electricity are about 3.5 tonnes.[13] As the super-rich achieve ever more preposterous fortunes, they simply run out of stuff to spend it on and sink their incomes and wealth into bigger, more polluting projects like space travel and yachts the size of small cities. As a result, climate change and the ruinous consequences it will have for the entire planet becomes harder to avoid. This risk would be greatly mitigated by reducing the fortunes of the super-rich.

Similarly, the UK's acute housing crisis provides a further example of a problem that could be alleviated by reducing inequality. Where the supply of (often critical) products or services is finite, there is a risk that extreme concentrations of incomes and wealth enables the super-rich to buy more than they need while others have too little. Research from housing charities suggests that there are over 200,000 UK households experiencing the worst forms of homelessness (such as sleeping in cars or sheds, as well as on the streets).[14] Over 1 million people are on social housing waiting lists, and the proportion of people aged 35–44 living in rented accommodation has nearly tripled since the mid 1990s (28 per cent in 2020 compared to just 10 per cent in the mid-1990s).[15]

At the same time, research from the Resolution Foundation suggests that around 190,000 individuals disproportionately concentrated at the top of the income distribution own at least four 'buy-to-let' properties.[16] A further 61,000 have at least two 'second homes' (i.e. properties that they do not continuously let out to another household but use as holiday or country retreats).[17] There are a number of factors behind the housing crisis. But the small number of rich people able to limit the supply by buying multiple properties, helping to drive prices to a level unaffordable for many others in the process, is an example of the dysfunction resulting from extreme concentrations of income and wealth. If they were not hoarding such a disproportionate share of homes, it is likely that availability would increase, costs would reduce and a pathway to home ownership might open up for many more people.

There is also substantial evidence linking the level of inequality within a society, which is exacerbated by the extremely high income and wealth levels of the super-rich, to the prevalence of socio-economic problems, including lower social mobility, more widespread mental health problems, increased obesity and a higher homicide rate.[18] These problems tend to be worse when inequality is higher. The reasons for this are harder to pin down, but increased status anxiety and insecurity resulting from the existence of extremes of wealth and income is one hypothesis.

This chapter previously discussed how heightened inequality could encourage unsustainable spending and debt levels, on the basis that wider gaps in society create pressure on those falling behind to keep up with those who have pulled ahead. In the same way, it makes sense that in more unequal societies, those same households might feel greater stress relating to a sense of failure or inadequacy that comes from lacking the degree of material prosperity enjoyed by others, leading to mental health problems and issues with coping mechanisms like alcohol, drugs or junk food.

Similarly, even those who ostensibly benefit from inequality by being relatively better off compared to others might feel more paranoid or insecure about their prosperity, given that they have further to fall in a more unequal society. Wider differences in material prosperity and living standards potentially weaken empathy at both ends of the spectrum, fostering crime, resentment and fear.

While the precise reasons for the relationship between inequality and health and social problems will no doubt continue to be debated, perhaps the important point is that there are good grounds to think that more ambitious redistribution and pre-distribution would have positive long-term by-products in terms of alleviating these problems.

Meeting the challenges of the future requires effective taxation of the super-rich

Significant public investment will be required to address the major challenges presented by environmental and societal change. This creates a further socio-economic argument for taxing extreme incomes and wealth more effectively.

Preventing dangerous levels of climate change and the flooding, droughts, food shortages, conflict and mass migration that it is unleashing will require trillion dollar investments. For the UK to remain on track to reach net zero greenhouse gas emissions by 2050 will necessitate something like £100 billion worth of investment, beyond that already committed, in the 2020s alone, according to expert estimates. This will not all be financed by the government, but it is estimated that around 37–41 per cent of the funding committed or proposed for net zero projects in the 2020s will come from public investment.[19] Government is an obvious source of funding for many of the necessary measures that remain unfunded, like support for green technologies and improvements to the energy efficiency of buildings. The benefits to society of avoiding critical levels of global warming and the ensuing chaos provide a robust long-term business case for these kinds of investment, but governments will need sustainable tax revenue streams to fund the repayment costs.

Similarly, as people live longer, countries will have to support a much larger number of people through longer retirements with increased health care and social care costs. At the same time, an ageing population with a lower proportion of working-age people will find it harder to generate economic growth. Research from the IMF has estimated that in the US, tax revenues will have to rise by 11 per cent by 2050 if current levels of support for older people are to be maintained without spending cuts elsewhere, while the required increase ranges from 14 per cent to 28 per cent across different European countries.[20]

The cost of controlling the Covid pandemic and supporting populations through the crisis has also created unforeseen long-term costs for economies in terms of servicing the increased debt that governments took on to strengthen health care systems and protecting the incomes of those unable to work. With regard to meeting this challenge, the vast potential resource that the excess wealth of the super-rich represents is already becoming difficult to ignore. In addition to the calls from the IMF discussed earlier in the chapter, proposals for wealth taxes on very large fortunes have been put forward in multiple different countries and in some, such as Spain,

Argentina and Bolivia, different forms of wealth tax have been implemented or extended, with the express purpose of addressing the economic hangover from Covid.[21]

In the face of these challenges, the alternatives to taxing the super-rich are essentially (a) crossing our fingers, and hoping for implausible levels of economic growth or some kind of miraculous technological breakthrough that enables us to reverse the ageing process or colonise the moon; or (b) getting the funding from cuts to other public services.

If the second option seems superficially attractive, it's worth noting how hard this can be and the disastrous impact that such cuts can have. In France, efforts to raise the state pension age to 64 resulted in several months of protests – including many that descended into serious violence – involving millions of demonstrators.[22] In Great Britain, cuts to public services and social security coincided with 335,000 excess deaths in the period from 2010 to 2018, according to the University of Glasgow, emphasising the serious repercussions that reducing people's income or access to care and support can have.[23] One of the most high-profile cuts, the denial of additional support payments to families receiving tax credits or Universal Credit for more than two children, means around 250,000 more UK children were living in poverty as of 2023 than would otherwise be the case.[24]

These are direct consequences of our failure to tax the super-rich fairly, sensibly and sufficiently. Environmental, demographic and other emerging challenges are putting pressure on governments' capacity to deliver public services that are critical to maintaining and raising living standards. The extent to which we deal with them will be determined by our willingness to tackle extreme concentrations of income and wealth. In this respect, our tolerance of the super-rich represents a major threat to socio-economic prosperity.

The economic case for inequality relies on myths about the super-rich

Of course, the extent to which members of the public, and even policymakers, engage with the topics in this chapter is understandably limited. Relative international differences in income distributions, the marginal propensity to consume, and the relationship between economic inequality and health and social problems are not what normal people talk about day to day. They are not the sort of issues that energise a radio phone-in, or attract comments below a blog article, or prompt a standing ovation when mentioned at a politician's campaign rally.

Research and data provide assurances of the economic benefits of tackling the problem of the super-rich, and this is a key part of the case for action. But it is also important to create a persuasive narrative that makes sense of the state of the world. The mythologisation of the super-rich by politicians and commentators who are essentially pro-inequality tells a powerful story of why bolder attempts at redistribution or pre-distribution present an unacceptable risk.

According to this narrative, the super-rich play a critical, irreplaceable and fragile role as wealth creators. They have the capacity to accumulate huge incomes and wealth wherever they are based and the mobility to go more or less wherever they like. Thus, if they perceive a particular policy regime to be unfavourable to their interests, they will move to somewhere more hospitable, resulting in economic losses for their original location. But there is also a persuasive, empowering – and, critically – more accurate account of how prosperity is created. Put simply, it is a collective and collaborative process driven by the combined efforts of society as a whole, rather than something that is bestowed upon us by a tiny elite. Thus, the rewards should be shared more evenly. The next chapter will set out an argument to this effect, showing how the supposedly unique talents, mobility and importance to wider economic prosperity of the super-rich are wildly overstated.

4
Our Mis-Placed Deference to the Super-Rich

The previous chapter surveyed the strong evidence to suggest that an economy that puts more of the income and wealth captured by the super-rich into the hands of those in the middle and at the bottom will be both more equal and richer in aggregate. But it's also useful to examine the debate about the economic importance of the super-rich specifically and the supposed need for policies that win their approval and serve their interests.

The socio-economic benefits of a more equal economy with more effective taxation of the super-rich represents one argument for a more even distribution of income and wealth. Importantly, this is complemented by evidence that the economic value of the super-rich is nowhere near proportionate to the vast share of total incomes and wealth that they enjoy, nor are they as impervious to redistributive or pre-distributive policies as pessimists determined to defend extreme inequality might argue. Thus, efforts to redistribute and pre-distribute can be undertaken with confidence.

The super-rich themselves (or more typically, the lobbyists, think tanks and politicians that they fund) say that if they are prevented from accumulating such vast fortunes, they will move their tax contribution, spending power and unique ability to start and run businesses or fill other important jobs to a different jurisdiction. Any economy that tries to do without them will fall apart.

The pathway to prosperity for countries, according to this argument, involves making themselves as attractive as possible to plutocrats and the global financial and business elite by lowering taxes on the super-rich and removing other mechanisms that enable a more even balance of income and wealth.

This notion of the super-rich as engines of economic success effectively assumes that (a) prosperity is generated by a tiny elite of god-like individuals, (b) there is a fixed number of these individuals, and their skills cannot be replicated or replaced and (c) the rest of us are so stupid, slovenly and drunk that we can't do anything worthwhile or productive without this elite class ordering us about.

Like many of the arguments against doing anything about the super-rich it betrays a pretty pessimistic and contemptuous view of 99 per cent of the population and it rather falls apart under scrutiny.

Excessive incomes and wealth are not essential or even especially helpful as an incentive and reward for productivity; the capacity and will of the super-rich to avoid measures designed at rebalancing their extreme riches are exaggerated; and they are far less critical to the economic success of the country than their mouthpieces would have us believe.

By its own logic, a pro-super-rich regime eventually disadvantages everyone

The first and most obvious flaw with an approach to wealth creation that effectively involves bending over backwards for the super-rich is that it is only going to give any individual economy an edge if no-one else copies it – and if it actually

worked, then other countries would have to be pretty stupid
not to do so.

By their own logic, policies like cutting taxes on very high
levels of income and wealth, or eliminating employment
rights and other pro equality measures as a means of generating economic success, are likely to lead to an international
'race to the bottom'. If these policies really did attract more
rich people and this in turn really did lead to the wider population also becoming richer, every other country would do
the same thing, with the result that none of them end up being
relatively more attractive or advantaged over the long-term.
Meanwhile, in each country those at the top would grab an
even bigger share of total incomes and wealth, and vital public
services would be starved of much-needed resources.

It is hard to believe that this would lead to the best standard of living for the widest number of people that we could
achieve with the resources we have available – and there is real
world evidence that proves that it doesn't. The average top rate
of tax in the OECD (Organisation for Economic Co-operation
and Development) group of advanced economies has declined
from 66 per cent in 1981 to 43 per cent in 2022.[1] Researchers from the London School of Economics analysing every tax
cut in 18 OECD member states over 50 years found that while
they had helped the richest 1 per cent grab a bigger share of
total national income, they had no significant effect on economic growth in that country.[2]

Money isn't all that motivates people

The view that money is the supreme motivating factor for
people carrying out important roles is also simplistic from an
economic perspective. Indeed, when used to inform recruitment or retention strategies it can be lazy and wasteful.

Research into CEO pay suggests that the main financial motivation for chief executives does not derive from material concerns (e.g. buying a bigger car or yacht) but with being fairly rewarded for doing a good job.[3] Their perception of fairness is in turn shaped by the pay of other CEOs. If taxation, employment or business governance policies changed – not to mention stakeholder expectations, including those of workers, shareholders and the general public – the going rate for those at the top would fall over time and the executives, entrepreneurs and other high earners would accept this, provided the rewards they accumulate remained broadly in line with their peers.

The interest in relative rather than absolute pay is consistent with the view that the overriding motivation for people in high-earning roles is mostly non-financial – indeed much research on CEO pay suggests that incentive payments for hitting performance targets can override their previous intrinsic motivation for taking on the job.[4] The opportunity to do challenging and engaging work that generates personal prestige, respect or admiration from others is often more important than the rewards on offer. If lucrative professions no longer led to millionaire- or billionaire-level pay-outs but continued to generate these non-financial rewards, they would remain attractive.

A useful way to think of this is to compare the richest entrepreneurs and business leaders with other multi-millionaires in sports or entertainment. While sports stars are obviously keen to secure the best pay they can get – top footballers from all over the world don't move to Saudi Arabia out of fascination with ancient Islamic art and the country's intricate water supply system – it's also absolutely daft to suggest that if the rewards for playing elite sports were less, they simply wouldn't bother. Nobody seriously thinks that if taxes were higher Lionel Messi would decide that all the effort wasn't worth it, and retrain as an estate agent. The enormous financial rewards available to a grand-slam-winning tennis player aren't the only reason Roger Federer preferred a successful multi-decade career at the pinnacle of the sport to the steady stability of life as a ticket collector on Switzerland's world-leading railway network. It was their competitive spirit and love of their respective sports, rather than money, that were the driving forces in their career

The same principle applies to Bill Gates or Elon Musk. The challenge of reaching the absolute top level of business, finance, law or other well-rewarded professions requires competition with other ambitious and capable individuals. Success in these industries commands significant status. It provides the opportunity to work on complex and challenging projects that the post-holder has considerable authority to shape in line with their interests and priorities. This work enables the development of very high-level expertise and will typically have significant impacts on a wide number of people (managing a large company; overseeing their audit process; or leading a major legal case with wider ramifications for example). Whether or not it leads to enormous financial rewards has little bearing on any of these hugely important motivating factors. Even if starting a company like Microsoft or Tesla had not enabled Gates or Musk to accumulate greater wealth than the populations of entire countries, they would still command attention from heads of state, celebrities and the world's media.

The status, influence, expertise, autonomy and intellectual stimulation that typically accompany the roles that make people super-rich are sufficient incentive to ensure that capable candidates would continue to come forward as entrepreneurs, CEOs, bankers and lawyers, even if those posts didn't generate the extreme levels of income and wealth that they do today. Therefore policymakers timidity towards measures that would reduce these extreme levels to more reasonable amounts is unnecessary (particularly if they could implement such measures in a co-ordinated fashion on an international basis).

The super-rich are not as footloose and mobile as claimed

The argument that we don't need to let people capture such a huge share of incomes and wealth to motivate or reward success is also supported by substantial research and analysis regarding the mobility of the super-rich. Their ability or desire to up sticks and relocate in a more pliant jurisdiction if their home country becomes braver in standing up to extreme concentrations of income and wealth is frequently cited as an argument against redistribution or pre-distribution. But it is asserted with much greater certainty than is warranted by the evidence.

The risk of losing top executives to overseas competitors is often used to justify the multi-million-pound pay packages commonly awarded to business leaders. But if this were actually the case, every capable CEO would already be working in America where executive pay levels dwarf those in every other country. At $14.5 million, the median pay of a CEO of the S&P 500 companies in America is around three times that of the median pay for the CEOs of the biggest companies in the UK, Canada, France or Germany.[5]

Despite this, it is incredibly rare for successful, skilled executives from other countries to relocate to America. A 2020 analysis of the biggest firms in the US found that just 11 per cent of firms had a CEO from outside the US.[6] Among this small proportion, over a third had come to America either as children or students and most of the remainder had worked for their employer from a young age and risen through the ranks. It was overwhelmingly not the case that they were recruited as fully fledged executives from lower-paying companies, like star footballers transferring from one club from another.

A similar High Pay Centre study found that fewer than 1 per cent of the CEOs of the world's biggest businesses had been poached from an international rival.[7] The overwhelming majority of companies appointed a leader from their home country, who had worked their way up through the organisation over time. This makes sense – even businesses that operate globally strongly identify with the country where they are headquartered. The domestic market almost always constitutes a disproportionately large component of the customer, employee and investor populations, as well as exerting an outsized regulatory influence on multiple business practice issues, such as corporate governance structure or investor relations. As such, potential business leaders who understand the domestic corporate culture have huge advantages over international rivals.

This again suggests that paying business leaders vast sums of money in order to attract and retain their services is frequently unnecessary. For the most part they would not be able to land similar roles elsewhere.

For bankers, lawyers, other high-earning professionals or entrepreneurs starting their own businesses, the risk of relocation is similarly overstated. Looking at the UK as a case study, while the finance sector and related industries in Britain undoubtedly draw on an international workforce, the reasons for the sector's strength and the UK's attractiveness as a business destination to which companies recruit overseas workers are numerous. These include the (hitherto) stable political and economic environment; the expertise and infrastructure relating to finance and related professions in the City of London;

the English language, which is the international language of business, and widely spoken as a second language, enabling foreigners to settle more easily; and a location in a time zone between both Asia and North America making it easier to do business with both markets over the course of a working day. It would be deeply irresponsible for any business to ignore these factors in favour of relocating somewhere where they can pay their top staff even more (at a considerable cost to the business). The suggestion that these strengths would disappear if Britain adopted a braver approach to tackling extreme concentrations of income and wealth, and that the supposedly critical highly skilled workforce would flee overseas reflects a lack of confidence in the country, a lack of patriotism even, and should not be uncritically accepted.

Higher taxes don't necessarily drive the super-rich overseas

The contention that the mobility of the super-rich and their sensitivity to efforts to reduce their vast incomes and wealth is overstated is also borne out by much of the research on taxation.

A 2020 summary of historic research into the effects of tax policy on migration, concluded that while a number of studies confirm evidence of rich people making location decisions based on tax considerations, this is subject to important caveats. Firstly, most research is concentrated on particular professions or geographies.[8] The authors observed that there was not systematic evidence that tax rates have a consistent impact on the location decisions of rich people generally.

Indeed, there are many examples of efforts to tax the super-rich more effectively that have been successfully implemented without the predicted negative consequences. When the UK reformed taxes on non-domiciled (non-dom) residents, meaning non-doms who had been in the UK for over 15 years would now have to pay taxes on overseas income, regardless of whether they brought it into the country, the proportion of those affected who chose to emigrate was estimated to be less than 5 per cent – a tiny number considering their post tax income declined by 18 per cent on average.[9] While the rates of millionaires and billionaires leaving Norway did increase significantly in response to a wealth tax increase in 2022, the rate of exit would need to have been 15 times higher than it actually was to have offset the increased revenue for public services that the tax increase achieved.[10]

Second, the 2020 analysis also found evidence that taxation is only one of a number of drivers of where rich people choose to live. Higher top rates of income tax across 12 high income economies cited in the analysis had no positive correlation with lower numbers of high earning foreign workers in the country, suggesting that high tax rates are not incompatible with attracting and retaining highly-skilled migrants. As a determinant of location decisions, tax considerations are dominated by other factors like the quality of infrastructure and public services; or recreation and leisure opportunities.

This is not a particularly surprising finding. Perhaps the single, defining characteristic of the super-rich is that they can afford not to have to make decisions based on cost. Just as they choose to shop in Harrods or Fortnum & Mason and drive a Ferrari or a Bentley, even though they could fulfil their nutritional needs more cost effectively at Aldi or Lidl and travel from A to B just as efficiently in a Nissan Micra, so they choose to live in Paris, London or New York even though rural Bulgaria would be cheaper. It might even be the case that higher rates of tax on the super-rich and the broader improvements to public services and facilities that they could fund would make a country *more* desirable to affluent people. As we have shown in previous chapters, those at the very top could still maintain a very high standard of living even if they paid a bit more in tax. It would hardly be surprising, therefore, if many were willing to do so in order to live in a cleaner, healthier, happier, more prosperous and stable society.

The risk of losing tax and investment overseas can be significantly mitigated

Of course, it is one thing to say that the risk of driving the super-rich overseas is exaggerated in order to protect their outsized share of national income and wealth. It is another to say that there is no risk at all.

One only has to look at the European Union's court cases with the likes of Apple and Google over their tax contribution in Europe, or the revelations in the Panama and Paradise papers exposing the vast wealth held in tax havens, to recognise that, whether by their location decisions or through the cunning and criminality of their business, investment and accountancy practices, big corporations and the super-rich can be highly adept at protecting their enormous riches from efforts to secure them for public services. Any attempt to achieve a more even balance of incomes and wealth would have to overcome this – but there are grounds to think it is an eminently achievable task.

First, higher taxes or other inhibitors of extreme concentrations of income and wealth, do not create some kind of chemical force that instantly propels super-rich individuals or their assets and income streams to other jurisdictions. It is a choice by those individuals (and their advisers) to hoard resources for themselves, even when they already have more than most people could ever dream of, rather than to use them to help society.

It is perhaps understandable that people in a position to do this might convince themselves that they genuinely deserve the money more than the public services that their taxes might fund, or the lower-paid workers who would benefit if they took a bigger slice of corporate profits, but it is not inevitable or universal. The 'Patriotic Millionaires' campaign of super-rich individuals committed to paying higher taxes and working towards a more equal society has been prominent in the US and has now started to campaign internationally as well. The UK's 'Fair Tax Mark' is awarded to businesses that commit to complying with the spirit as well as the letter of tax laws and pay a fair amount of tax. There have also been several well-targeted campaigns around the tax and pay practices of leading businesses and individuals that have forced them to adopt a more progressive approach.

It is not utopian to think that a more condemnatory attitude to the super-rich, and a more celebratory one towards those who accept that there is such a thing as 'enough' might encourage a more compliant approach towards tax or other policies and practices designed to achieve a more proportionate balance of incomes and wealth, borne either of a desire to avert public criticism or simply because it's the humane and compassionate thing to do.

Second, there is no reason to be unambitious or pessimistic about our capacity to tax the super-rich effectively. There are plenty of taxes that are hard to avoid legally. Physical assets like properties cannot be relocated. High-paying jobs have to be taxed in the country where they are being done. Foreign income cannot be remitted to the UK without incurring UK taxation, even for those with non-domiciled status.

There are further steps that governments could take to make it harder for the globally mobile to escape paying taxes. A research paper from the London School of Economics suggests toughening the requirements necessary to claim UK residency, including potentially requiring anyone wanting to claim non-residence to sell their UK home.[11] This would be a serious and significant disincentive to avoid paying taxes due from residents that anybody in the top 1 per cent could easily afford to pay. Similarly, introducing exit taxes on super-rich emigrants, such as a capital gains tax on the assumed value of their gains, effectively treating them as if they had sold the assets at the point of emigration, would both remove the incentive to emigrate for those who have made large capital gains, and ensure a tax contribution was paid, even from those that did choose to emigrate. This would be a totally reasonable measure in terms of essentially ensuring that people pay tax in the UK on wealth they accumulate in the country and would bring the UK in line with other countries such as Canada and Norway.

Third, it should be emphasised once again that extreme concentrations of income and wealth are a problem the world over. There are virtually no countries that could not achieve a significant uplift in living standards if their incomes and wealth were distributed more evenly. To the extent that it exists, the global mobility of the super-rich creates an argument for countries to work together to eliminate tax havens and to prevent a 'race to the bottom' between countries. There are plenty of examples of governments reaching agreements on topics from the banning of the toxic chlorofluorocarbons that damage the ozone layer to the corporation tax floor (which commits signatories to a corporation tax rate of at least 15 per cent), so that individual states can confidently commit to better social and environmental protections without worrying that other nations might seek to steal business from them by adopting laxer standards.[12] It would be totally feasible to secure similar agreements to prevent the super-rich from capturing an excessive share of aggregate income and wealth. In terms of global living standards, there could be few more worthwhile diplomatic initiatives.

Fourth, excessive incomes and wealth cannot be spirited away to the Cayman Islands or other tax havens if they never reach the super-rich in the first place. Challenges associated with redistribution are not an argument for just accepting massively unequal and inefficient concentrations of money and assets, they instead strengthen the case for pre-distributive measures that would mean that these resources accrue directly to the 99 per cent instead of the super-rich, circumventing some of the need for taxation. Mechanisms discussed in subsequent chapters, including stronger trade unions, profit-sharing requirements or maximum highest to lowest earner pay limits could all have this effect

Finally, while this book rejects the claim that a meaningful rebalancing of existing concentrations of income and wealth cannot be achieved, it is important to note the really terrible implications for democracy and the character of people who have economic power in society if it were correct.

If societies take the democratic view that their aggregate wealth is created collectively, and that the incomes and wealth of those at the very top should be shared more evenly, then that is what should happen. The possibility that the super-rich are powerful enough to prevent the democratically expressed wishes of society from being fulfilled is a strange argument to deploy in their favour. Similarly, the super-rich are put in charge of businesses managing large numbers of people. They control access to finance, business advice, and legal and accountancy work for both the private sector and governments. What does the assertion that they would vigorously resist greater pre-distribution or redistribution of their vast income and wealth say about the character of the people controlling these vital functions? If they really are so venal, and so impervious to democratically instituted laws that apply to everybody else, that they are willing and able to escape their contribution towards better public services – to help sick people get treatment, to give children a better chance in life, or to protect and keep safe in those in danger or need – even though it wouldn't really affect their super-rich status, that might on one level weaken the argument for taxation of the super-rich. But in a much more important way it strengthens the notion that their existence is a huge problem that needs to be addressed.

The super-rich don't contribute disproportionately to public services and investment

Finally, even if the super-rich were not willing to accept reductions of their incomes and wealth to more proportionate levels and were able to relocate to different international jurisdictions, their importance to wider prosperity has again been exaggerated considerably.

For example, the taxes paid by the super-rich are often used to justify their socio-economic importance, but their tax contribution is a function of outsized inequality. It doesn't mean that extreme concentrations of income and wealth are necessary to fund public services. In the US, the Institute of Taxation and Economic Policy (ITEP) estimates that the top 1 per cent by income contributed about 24 per cent of tax revenues, compared to the ITEP's estimate of 21 per cent of total incomes accruing to the top 1 per cent.[13] Bearing in mind that everyone in this group has at least several hundred thousand dollars-worth of income and could easily afford to contribute more while maintaining a very high standard of living, the fact that they pay tax worth little more than the share of income they accumulate makes their contribution pretty meagre.

Similarly, in the UK, an analysis by the Institute for Fiscal Studies (IFS) looking at tax payments covering around three quarters of UK tax revenues, including the four biggest taxes in terms of revenue, found that the richest 10 per cent of households contributed around 30 per cent of these revenues in the tax year 2016/17.[14] The World Inequality Database records the top 10 per cent (of individuals) by income in the UK capturing 36 per cent of total incomes in 2017. The IFS notes that their analysis excludes some smaller taxes paid disproportionately by the super-rich and also that it becomes harder to accurately capture the incomes and tax of those at the top of the distribution because surveying such a small group of people in a representative way is more challenging. Therefore, their figures are probably a considerable underestimate. However, as a very approximate indicator of the proportion of taxes contributed by the super-rich compared to their income or wealth, they don't suggest an especially generous contribution. Most reasonable people would expect very rich people, who have a lot more money, to pay a higher proportion of tax, as well as a higher absolute amount. Taking a proportion of income or wealth from a poorer person is going to have a much more negative impact on their living standards than taking the same proportion from a much richer one. The relevant consideration governing whether someone is making a fair tax contribution or not is how much they have left over *after* paying their tax, and whether this leaves them fairly rewarded and incentivised for the work they do. In the case of the super-rich, the evidence suggests that they do not pay an outsized amount of tax, and there is clearly scope for them to pay a lot more while still maintaining a very high standard of living.

The underwhelming tax contribution of the super-rich is also visible in research on the billionaires who dominate the UK rich list. Fewer than half of the top 20 entrants on the rich list are lifelong UK residents – only 3 of the 20 entrants appear on the list of the UK's top 20 highest taxpayers and only one of those who has moved to the UK, tech entrepreneur Alex Gerko, features on the list of top taxpayers.[15] Making Britain attractive to foreign oligarchs doesn't appear to have helped our public finances much. Conversely, the top taxpayers are overwhelmingly billionaires with roots in the UK, highlighting how if your home, family and business assets are located somewhere, the ability and desire to escape making a tax contribution in that country is limited and we should not be afraid to make an effort to capture a little more of the excessive wealth of those in this group.

The vitally important additional point to emphasise about taxes, and also the amounts that the super-rich invest in the economy, is that the share of the total that they contribute results from the very high share of all incomes and wealth that they control. Obviously, if one group of people has a disproportionately huge amount of money compared to everybody else, they are also going to both pay more tax and make more investments. This doesn't mean society relies on those at the top to fund public services and business growth, and that it wouldn't happen without them. If the super-rich and the companies they own and run paid their workers more, then those workers would be able to afford to make a greater tax contribution and to build up savings that could subsequently be invested. Reducing extreme income and wealth concentration would thus mean that tax contributions and investment opportunities would be spread more evenly rather than disappearing altogether. This is borne out by the research on 'savings gluts' cited in the previous chapter, showing that the vast increase in savings of the rich 1 per cent in the US since the 1980s was accompanied by 'dis-saving' by poorer households and government, meaning that overall investment actually fell during the period over which the super-rich increased their wealth most aggressively.[16]

The super-rich are not uniquely and irreplaceably capable and competent

In terms of the less tangible skills that the super-rich contribute to societies alongside their financial contribution, again their importance and irreplaceability are overstated. People are not born with an innate capability to be a tech entrepreneur, banker, CEO or lawyer. While some individuals may have particular general attributes that make them potentially more suited to certain roles than others, the main determinant of the number of people capable of doing this type of work is the number that have been given the necessary training, confidence and experience. We can expand this pool, rather than just assume that its size is fixed and that we are unavoidably dependent on those already within it.

In 2021, about 19,000 UK students graduated with a law degree.[17] Figures from the Higher Education Statistics Authority show that there are nearly 10,000 graduates of UK universities from the class of 2020/21 working in the finance industry.[18] There are over 400,000 people in the UK studying for a degree in business or management.[19] These numbers equate to tens of thousands of prospective lawyers or bankers or business leaders and entrepreneurs entering the jobs market every year. (That's before one considers that graduates in other disciplines or people who didn't go to university at all might also have the capability and aspiration to reach high-earning roles.)

This contrasts with a few thousand people in the very highest-earning professions at any one time – for example, as of early 2023 there are around 600 FTSE 350 executives (average pay of £2 million), and close to 3,000 partners at the 'magic circle' law firms (£1.9 million) or big four accountancy firms (£911k), while the most recent figures suggest there are about 4,000 UK-based bankers paid over £1 million.[20]

Assuming that people doing degrees in business, finance, law and related professions want to reach the top of those industries, there is very obviously a mismatch between the limited demand for people to fill the small number of senior roles and the huge supply of candidates with relevant qualifications and the theoretical ability to do the job. This again suggests we should not fear threats by the super-rich to quit the country. While those at the top of high earning professions must have progressed further in their careers than their peers, this is often down to connections, encouragement, subjective preferment by others and outright luck. It doesn't mean they have some unique quality that businesses and economies can't cope without, and that thousands of other similarly-qualified people don't also possess.

In a functioning market we would also expect the excessive supply of potential top professionals relative to demand to exert irresistible downward pressure on top pay.

The fact that it fails to do so suggests two possibilities. First, that qualifications in finance and related subjects and subsequent professional development are failing spectacularly to equip students and young professionals with the necessary capabilities for career progression. Thus, as a result, the actual pool of potential top executives, lawyers, bankers and entrepreneurs is still very small and the few people capable of filling these roles are able to command huge fees. If this were the case, it would be really troubling and necessitate pretty far-reaching reform of universities and employment and skills policy.

The alternative and far likelier explanation is that the governance and management processes that set top pay levels are deeply flawed, leading to vastly excessive pay awards.

The boards and remuneration committees that determine pay-outs for top professionals are affected by significant biases and conflicts of interest, conscious or otherwise, that make their judgements on pay highly fallible. Risk aversion and hassle aversion are powerful motivators for anyone involved in setting pay (particularly for people spending their company's money rather than their own). It's much easier to recruit or retain a supposed superstar banker or lawyer rather than identify a high potential, less costly but lesser-known alternative. The boards and pay committees are also typically populated by current or former high earners who themselves benefit or have benefited from a culture of excess top pay. At worst, they have an explicit vested interest in pushing up the pay for other senior professionals because it indirectly influences the going rate for their own work. At best, they have an unconscious and instinctive bias in favour of generous pay awards because the argument that the people who have reached those positions are uniquely capable, and need to be paid whatever it takes to attract and retain their services, provides a satisfactory explanation for their own high pay.

These biases and conflicts of interest totally distort the pay-setting process in business, finance and other top professions, leading to pay levels grossly elevated beyond what we might expect in a functional free market where decisions are made by objective and disinterested market participants.

Reforming these governance processes – giving the company's workforce a democratic say in who sits on the remuneration committee; making corporations and financial institutions more accountable over their pay practices – would help working people secure a fairer share of the wealth that their labour generates for these companies. In the unlikely event of that resulting in a mass resignation of business leaders, bankers and other high earners, this ought not to be a problem for economies where educational institutions and employers are providing the huge number of people who would like to fulfil those roles with the training, confidence and opportunities to do so.

The economic case against the super-rich mirrors the moral case

The uncritical attitude of remuneration committees towards high earners reflects many of the common misconceptions about the super-rich discussed in this chapter. From an economic perspective, their value and importance are overstated and a more even distribution of income and wealth would be a better outcome.

However, we do not and should not make policy decisions purely on cold economic logic. Doing what is morally right matters too.

Resources should be allocated in a way that maximises living standards but also rewards factors like hard work or socially useful activity fairly and proportionately. The next chapter will show how the current income and wealth levels of the super-rich are not only unjustifiable from an economic perspective, they are also badly at odds with this principle of fair, proportionate reward that any healthy society ought to reflect.

5
Unearned Income and Wealth

The fact that the super-rich are not as unique or irreplaceable as they claim should strengthen the economic arguments for tackling extreme concentrations of income and wealth. But it also hints at a more fundamental reason for action. The super-rich do not work that much harder than anybody else and they do not generate that much value for wider society.

In general, their success is hugely contingent on the exclusive opportunities they have been given, their ability to profit from the hard work of others and their exploitation of ownership of assets like property, patents or businesses where immense wealth accrues to them simply as a result of their power and positioning.

Put simply, they do not deserve their extraordinary riches. As well as boosting living standards for the majority, reducing extreme concentrations of income and wealth would have the added bonus of reflecting more accurately the value and contribution of the work that different people do.

The super-rich don't work much harder than the rest of us, if they work at all

An Essex University analysis of the richest people in the UK by income found that 15 per cent of people in the top 1 per cent received their income without having to work at all.[1] This equates to tens of thousands of people, each making hundreds of thousands of pounds or more every year, effectively just sitting on the sofa (or on a beach somewhere) waiting for rental payments from their property portfolio or dividends from the companies they invest in to pile up. The same analysis suggested that within the top 0.01 per cent of the population – around 5,000 people with average incomes in excess of £5 million – only around 60 per cent of their income came from earnings from work, with the remainder rolling in from the investments that they own.

The argument that the super-rich deserve their immense incomes because of how hard they work is obviously a bit nonsensical in these cases. However, even in the case of those who do work for their money, the amount of work they do is nowhere near enough to justify prevailing income differences.

Government data suggests that the top 1 per cent of earners in the UK work 60 hours a week on average.[2] A detailed study of CEO working hours in the US similarly concluded that they spent an average of 62.5 hours a week at work.[3] This represents a more demanding schedule than the 37 hours a week that is the average for the UK working population as a whole. But it means than someone at the threshold for the top 1 per cent of UK earners makes more than five times as much as the median UK worker, for working less than twice as hard. A FTSE 100 CEO works 1.7 times more than the median UK full-time earner but is paid 118 times as much.

Extreme wealth usually comes from family, connections or an advantaged upbringing

Clearly, then, there is no basis for thinking that extreme concentrations of income and wealth result from proportionate levels of hard work or effort. The fortunes (an apposite term in every sense of the word) of the super-rich are more plausibly explained by their privileged backgrounds and powerful connections.

Looking at the absolute wealthiest people in Britain, 9 of the top 20 richest entrants on the 2023 Sunday Times Rich List (with net wealth of between £5 billion and £28 billion) are on the list either as a result of directly inheriting their wealth, or inheriting the businesses that ultimately generated it.[4] On the 2022 list, the top 20 contained an additional 4 billionaires from the former Soviet Union, who happened to be in the right place at the right time to invest in privatised state assets that proved key to their enrichment. (Three of these four were placed under sanctions in the UK because of their links to the Russian regime, in the aftermath of the invasion of Ukraine.)

Self-help books and LinkedIn influencers regularly promote the habits of highly successful people that others should seek to copy – the backgrounds of UK billionaires suggests that 'inheriting vast business empires' and 'befriending Vladimir Putin' should feature prominently on their lists.

It is not ideal that a tiny number of people can enjoy such vast fortunes, far beyond what anyone could ever need or even spend, while so many people in the world have so little. When those who hold enormous wealth do so as a result of accident of birth or powerful connections, it is doubly annoying.

Even in the case of those on the rich list who are supposedly self-made, a glance at their biographies shows the major role that circumstances have played in many cases in their wealth accumulation. Vacuum cleaner manufacturer Sir James Dyson (second on the rich list with £23 billion) was educated at one of the most expensive boarding schools in the UK.[5] Hedge fund owner Michael Platt (tenth on the rich list, with £10 billion) has recounted being taught how to invest on the stock market aged 14 by his grandmother.[6]

Analysis by the Sutton Trust found that of the total educated in the UK, 48 per cent of FTSE 100 CEOs and 54 per cent of entrants on the Sunday Times Rich List were privately educated, compared to just 7 per cent of the population.[7] Research has also shown that children with parents in elite, high-earning occupations are much more likely to enter those professions themselves – for example, the children of lawyers are 17 times more likely than average to become lawyers, while the children of people working in finance are 5 times more likely to enter the industry.[8] Intriguingly, the research also found that even within elite occupations and comparing people with similar levels of education, people from working-class backgrounds earn 16 per cent less than their peers who had privileged upbringings (with definitions of 'working class' and 'privileged' based on their parents' occupations).

This suggests that getting to the top of very high-earning professions depends a lot on the ability to relate to the disproportionately upper-class people already in those positions. That is obviously grossly unfair, and also endorses the economic arguments in the previous chapter: the super-rich are very often not super-rich because of their unique and irreplaceable talents that we must retain in Britain at any cost, but because they have the right accent, they move in the right circles and they have the right cultural reference points to ingratiate themselves at job interviews and around the office.

While the class system is often perceived as being uniquely British, in contrast to 'the American dream', which enables anyone to succeed in the US provided they work hard enough, analysis of American billionaires reveals a similarly important role for family wealth, connections and a privileged upbringing as the principal means of achieving super-rich status.

Forbes magazine's record of the 400 richest Americans identifies 31 per cent of entrants on the list as having inherited either the entirety of their fortune or the business and assets on which it is based.[9] This still leaves 69 per cent who are supposedly self-made, but *Forbes* categorises two thirds of this group as being from wealthy or affluent backgrounds. Examples include Jeff Bezos, who was able to start Amazon with a $250,000 loan from his stepfather, or Mark Zuckerberg, whose parents nurtured his interest in programming with private tuition in computing as an 11-year-old.[10]

Of course, not everybody who goes to private school or receives private tuition or gets a loan or business advice from their parents goes on to become a billionaire. Virtues like determination, initiative and ability have enabled these individuals to capitalise on their opportunities. But very many people are denied the opportunity. Being in possession of the head start offered by a six-figure parental loan or a family with extensive assets and knowledge in a particular industry is a more distinct defining characteristic than being capable, hard working or enterprising. These are traits that are not uniquely common to the super-rich and do not explain why they are super-rich. The most extensive talents and a dedicated work ethic cannot flourish outside the right environment. The luck, for want of a better word, of being born into favourable circumstances is completely critical to extreme income and wealth accumulation. Therefore, it is difficult to argue that such immense fortunes are earned or deserved.

Economic prosperity and business success are created collectively, not individually

Both the economic and moral excuses for inaction on the super-rich, come from telling ourselves the wrong story about how wealth and prosperity are created. We overrate the role of individual entrepreneurs or CEOs and underrate the collective and collaborative nature of wealth creation. Investors and executives are hugely dependent on the workers whose labour makes money for their businesses, and the collective resources provided by society as a whole and coordinated by the state for the benefit of those businesses.

Leading companies exemplify this tendency. Their CEOs are about the highest earners across the entire economy and a benchmark for the pay of other top executives and senior business managers. As we have noted, pay for a FTSE 100 CEO in the UK currently stands at £3.9 million while it is over $14 million for the CEO of an S&P 500 company in America.[11] These companies also generate huge profits which accrue to the super-rich to a vastly disproportionate degree – the FTSE 100 companies paid out around £120 billion in dividends and buybacks in 2022.[12]

The CEOs of large businesses are frequently profiled in media outlets. Stock market movement worth hundreds of millions, or even billions of pounds, occur on the basis of their job changes, with traders buying or selling shares depending on the appointment or removal of a supposedly good or bad CEO. This all contributes to a perception (conscious or otherwise) that companies are the embodiment of their CEOs and wholly dependent on their genius.

But as of early 2023, there is only one FTSE 100 CEO who actually founded their company. In America, founder CEOs are more commonplace, but still represent less than 4 per cent of the CEOs of the largest companies.[13] The remainder are professional managers who have been appointed to their role at historic businesses, rather than entrepreneurs who have built up an organisation from nothing. They have inherited an existing business infrastructure – a recognised brand, a loyal customer base, supply chains, business processes, factories, warehouses, equipment, and thousands of experienced colleagues throughout the world. Very often CEOs and other senior managers rake in vast pay-outs simply because they happen to be in post when geopolitical events create demand for products or services that their well-established companies are positioned to meet. For example, the FTSE 100 CEOs receiving the five biggest pay increases in 2022 included three bosses of oil and gas companies (BP, Shell and Centrica) that benefited from the increase in global oil and gas prices arising from geopolitical developments like the spike in demand after the Covid-19 pandemic and the disruption to supply caused by Russia's invasion of Ukraine.[14] Alongside them was the boss of arms manufacturer BAE Systems, whose share price jumped by around 55 per cent over the year after the invasion prompted governments across the world to increase defence spending.[15] The pay increase accruing to the four CEOs amounted to £16 million on top of the combined £19 million they received the previous year.

Similarly, a 2023 study from London Business School examining the effects of corporation tax cuts enacted by Donald Trump in the US again exemplifies how executives benefit from being in the right place at the right time. The tax cuts delivered a massive and sudden increase in the earnings of corporations because less tax had to be paid.[16] This meant CEOs smashed their performance targets far more easily than they would have otherwise done and raked in bigger bonuses, despite the fact that the earnings increase was nothing to do with them. The study estimated that the excess pay-outs accruing to the CEOs of the companies with the biggest windfall gains from the tax cuts amounted to about $170 million in total bonuses for the CEOs of around 500 companies. There were no apparent gains for the workers at those companies.

The role of luck as a driver of business success and executive pay awards does not mean that leadership is not important –

but people who are effectively private sector bureaucrats do not merit pay awards hundreds of times the pay of everybody else, just for maintaining and managing already functional organisations and being in the right place at the right time.

Even in the case of entrepreneurs starting from scratch, or successful managers who significantly increase a company's earnings or market value through genuine innovation, they will depend on colleagues to provide accurate and timely data, insights and advice to inform their decisions, and to possess the necessary competence and initiative to execute them.

Major decisions will also require input and approval from the entire board and, in well-run organisations, probably investors too, plus trade unions or other representatives of the workforce. This is a point that is overlooked by people who argue that, because the CEOs take decisions affecting companies worth billions, they deserve to be paid millions. No decision is taken in a vacuum and, in a large organisation, the executives are much more likely to be reliant on other people. As the chair of a major UK bank put it in a research interview for a High Pay Centre report examining the importance of executives to company performance: 'the bigger the system, the more it's the system that counts not the person on top of it'.[17]

Indeed, if one individual is able to significantly affect the value of the enterprise *without* carefully taking the advice of these different stakeholders, it is likely to be as a destroyer of wealth, rather than a creator. This is often a theme of corporate catastrophes. For example, analyses of the global financial crisis of the late 2000s have repeatedly found that the lack of checks and balances on the domineering personalities of CEOs like Fred Goodwin of RBS and Dick Fuld of Lehman Brothers were factors in the reckless risks taken by those organisations.[18] What this suggests is that, in general, people in the highest-earning roles either rely heavily on those around them or are not very good at their jobs. Either way, they probably do not deserve pay packages that are often hundreds of times the value of the salaries of the ordinary workers who keep their companies running.

Public money props up the super-rich

Beyond their dependence on lower-earning colleagues internally, super-rich business executives and investors are hugely dependent on direct and indirect support from government, including substantial amounts of public money, as an invaluable platform for their supposed success and consequent extreme income and wealth accumulation. Even firms synonymous with innovation, whose billionaire founders are held up as some of the most entrepreneurial capitalists in history, are much more reliant on the state than is commonly thought. The 'Good Jobs First' subsidy tracker in the US suggests that Tesla has had over $3 billion in public money through various loans and grants, helping Elon Musk to compete for the title of world's richest man.[19] The role of the state in funding the research into technologies successfully commercialised by companies such as Google and Apple has also been underplayed, relative to the profile of the entrepreneurs behind these companies, including several individuals who have gone on to achieve billionaire status.[20]

In the UK, it is probably quicker to list the major companies that don't benefit from massive government support than those that do. As we have noted, the FTSE 100 companies paid out over £1 billion to a few hundred executives in 2022, and over £100 billion to investors.[21] Reviewing the list of these companies shows just how central the state is to the generation of all this wealth. Government support and public money is critical to just about every sector in which the biggest British businesses operate.

In the extractive industries, the ability to win permits to mine or drill is key to success, and this ability depends on significant support from the UK government. Stories abound relating to UK ministers lobbying of foreign administrations regarding legal issues and exploration permits facing businesses including oil companies BP and Shell or mining conglomerate Rio Tinto.[22]

Similarly, UK defence and manufacturing firms operate almost in partnership with the UK state. The former Foreign Secretary Robin Cook noted that the chair of arms manufacturer BAE Systems 'appeared to have the key to the garden door to number 10 (Downing Street)' during his tenure.[23] The company famously benefited from UK government pressure on the Serious Fraud Office to drop an investigation into alleged bribes paid by BAE employees to Saudi Arabian officials.[24] BAE, FTSE 100 rival Rolls Royce and other arms manufacturers have between them over 50 paid staff embedded within the Ministry of Defence and a UK government body promoting defence exports as secondees.[25]

The value of the UK's banking sector is also propped up by the implicit understanding that bailouts similar to those undertaken in the aftermath of the financial crisis will be repeated if they run into major financial difficulties, with experts suggesting that this effective subsidy could be worth as much as £100 billion to 'too big to fail' UK banks.[26] This is critical to their ability to lavish million-pound pay awards on thousands of top staff and make huge dividend pay-outs to their investors.

Most of the UK's large retail and hospitality chains are supported indirectly with public money through in-work benefits to their staff. Without this they'd either have to significantly increase pay levels (thereby reducing their profitability) or maintain existing levels of productivity with a big element of their workforce struggling to cover their living costs and therefore tired, hungry, unwell and extremely stressed out. A 2021 report found that nearly 700,000 key workers, including hundreds of thousands of supermarket staff, were receiving in-work benefits via the Universal Credit system.[27]

The Covid-19 pandemic amplified this effect on a much wider scale, when at a time of economic crisis companies from across the economy were able to draw on public money to remain operational. 30 per cent of FTSE 350 companies benefited from direct subsidies, according to research from Aston University with some receiving as much as £150 million.[28] The direct support for businesses provided during the Covid crisis also understates the indirect effects. Most large businesses would have been devastated, with huge implications for their investors and top-earning staff, by the hit to the incomes of their customers, their suppliers and other stakeholders had the government not been there to provide support, even if they were not directly supported themselves.

The wider, indirect impact of the Covid support highlights the obvious dependence that the super-rich have on resources provided collectively by everybody else. They wouldn't be able to get rich without, for example, a healthy and educated workforce and customer base, roads and transport networks that provide the companies they own and run with a means of getting their products from place to place, or a police force and courts system that prevents or deters Mad Max-style motorcycle gangs from pillaging their property.

The super-rich and their companies do, in theory, contribute taxes towards the maintenance of these services and facilities. But again, it is important to return to this question of how these people become super-rich and whether it is down to some degree of hard work or genius proportionate to their level of income or wealth. When one thinks of how the living standards of anyone born in the UK or in other high-income countries have been achieved, it's clearly the luck of being born into a functional society that is of the most overwhelming importance rather than individual effort or intelligence. If Elon Musk, Jeff Bezos or Mark Zuckerberg had grown up in an environment where infrastructure, education, health care and the rule of law were more precarious, they would never have developed the personal capability to start world-leading companies, even if the lack of finance, resources, human capital, and political and economic stability did not make it completely impossible to do so in that kind of context anyway.

When individuals build a business that is so completely contingent on a functional wider society, it is illogical that they should accrue incomes and wealth far beyond the overwhelming majority of people who live in that society and co-create it, particularly when most of those people, purely by accident of birth, will never have the same opportunity to become super rich.

Super-rich status often reflects rewards for failure or mediocrity

Quite apart from the fact that the super-rich are essentially capitalising on the productivity of wider society to become super-rich, it is equally often the case that their achievements are often not the reward for doing anything especially impressive or socially useful.

The fact that figures mentioned previously like Fred Goodwin and Dick Fuld walked away from their disastrous tenures having made tens of millions of pounds or dollars for having crashed the economy was one of the most incendiary aspects of the banking crisis. Though these were particularly extreme examples of obscene rewards for abysmal performance, they are not especially unique. In recent years in the UK alone, executives at confectionery retailer Patisserie Valerie made nearly £3 million profit selling shares awarded as part of their incentive plans, shortly before the emergence of accountancy irregularities and the collapse of the company.[29] The CEO of the travel company Thomas Cook was paid £8.4 million over the course of his tenure, from his appointment in 2014 to the company's insolvency five years later.[30] Executives at outsourcing firm Carillion received £4 million in bonuses – on top of six-figure salaries – in 2017, just one year before the company was liquidated.[31]

Ironically, the CEOs who preside over major failures tend to be among those who accept the arguments made in the previous paragraphs – that there are limitations to their capabilities, they are reliant on the competence and judgements of their colleagues, and that their performance is greatly affected by the economic and political context in which they operate. Unfortunately, this is usually done inadvertently as part of an epic buck-passing exercise. The Thomas Cook CEO and his predecessors variously blamed the global economic crisis, the Icelandic ash cloud, the 2018 summer heatwave and the situation they inherited upon their appointment for the travel company's collapse at a Parliamentary Select Committee hearing in 2019.[32] In the aftermath of scandals like the interest rate manipulation abuses occurring at UK banks, or the phone hacking undertaken by News Corp journalists, senior figures at those companies offered the defence that they simply didn't know about the different practices taking place at the huge organisations they were running.[33] The CEO of Centrica, the owner of British Gas, professed to be 'disappointed, livid and gutted' when he found out – from journalists – about the practice of contractors breaking into vulnerable customers' homes to instal pre-payment meters, again pleading ignorance of what was going on at his own company.[34]

There is possibly an element of reasonableness to the defence that individual CEOs can't have oversight of thousands of colleagues simultaneously at all times. But it is completely hypocritical to accept enormous payments because of the awesome responsibility of running large and complex organisations, then effectively use their size and complexity to deny responsibility when things go wrong. Not all business leaders and other high-fliers find themselves in the position of having to explain the incongruity of their massive pay awards and the high-profile disasters that they've overseen. But that is less due to their brilliant judgement than the luck of wider circumstances not conspiring to make them look crooked or negligent in the way they did the executives of Thomas Cook, News Corp or the major banks. Some might get through their tenures without this being exposed too painfully, but none of them are the omnipotent deities they are portrayed and paid to be.

This point is borne out by more systematic research that found only a weak link between very high pay and company performance – indeed, a study of over 400 large companies in the US found that over a ten-year period, the companies with CEOs who received pay awards lower than the median for their sector over the period were likely to have performed better than those where pay awards were above the sector median![35] In the UK, a study looking at FTSE 350 directors' pay between 2000 and 2013 found that median directors' pay increased at twice the rate of median pre-tax profit for FTSE 350 companies and almost four times the rate of the market value of those companies.[36] During this period the typical pay of a FTSE 100 CEO more than doubled relative to that of the median UK worker, and it has remained constant at more than 100 times median full-time earnings ever since.[37]

In 2022, 97 per cent of FTSE 100 CEOs were paid over £1 million, and 87 per cent received at least £2 million around 14 times the earnings necessary to reach the top 1 per cent of UK earners.[38] Research showing that the difference between a good CEO and a bad one can be worth a significant amount of money to companies is sometimes used to justify the case for spending more to attract a good one, but this argument falls apart a bit when literally all CEOs are paid extraordinary sums and their pay doesn't really correlate with performance.

Super-rich status often reflects rewards for socially useless activity

Even in the case of executives and entrepreneurs who navigate their tenure while maintaining profitable businesses or meeting performance targets, this definition of business success should not be confused with being socially useful. Very frequently, the super-rich generate their fortunes from activities that do not particularly benefit society or, in some cases, actively damage it.

Looking at the UK rich list, the top 20 billionaires include 7 entrants whose fortune results wholly or in part from lucrative assets in the oil, gas and petrochemicals industry with its immensely destructive environmental footprint.[39] There are also entrants whose wealth or family wealth derives primarily from gambling and alcohol. In the US, the top 20 includes one major fossil fuel baron plus 2 entrants whose family wealth derives from the sale of confectionery products that contribute to major public health issues in a country where the population consumes on average two to three times the recommended amount of sugar per day, according to the

American Heart Association, and four out of ten people are obese.[40]

The top two wealthiest Americans, Jeff Bezos and Elon Musk, have both been criticised over the working conditions at their warehouses and factories.[41] Mark Zuckerberg, just outside the top ten, gets his wealth from social media behemoths like Facebook and Instagram, which have been strongly linked with significant increases in mental health problems among children and young people.[42]

This is not to take a puritanical view that people should be prohibited or even deterred from drinking alcohol, eating chocolate, gambling or using social media. The wealth generated from these activities demonstrates that people must be deriving some kind of pleasure from them, representing a form of social value against which to offset the costs. Even the fossil fuel industry is, on one level, meeting a demand for its products. At the same time, it would be hopelessly naïve to think that these vast and powerful corporations don't use their immense wealth and power in manipulative ways to influence consumers and policymakers in their favour and make money for their billionaire owners. In the case of products that are to varying degrees addictive, like alcohol, gambling, junk food or social media, which many consumers would probably like to use a lot less, this is doubly the case.

There is also, morally speaking, a world of difference between accepting the individual's right to gorge on a diet of Mars Bars and Heinekens, and enabling billionaires to accumulate obscene levels of wealth from products like these while passing the ensuing costs in terms of increased health problems or crime and anti-social behaviour on to wider society.

Furthermore, the examples from the rich list are not isolated instances of big businesses making huge amounts of money for the super-rich while imposing great costs on society. Research by the Schroders investment fund has estimated that around a third of the world's biggest companies would no longer be profitable if they themselves bore the costs of the social and environmental problems that emerge as by-products of their business (suggesting that the other two thirds would also see their profits considerably reduced).[43] This shows that even if we ignore the many reasons why we shouldn't attribute the perceived success of large businesses to their executives and owners, success in financial terms shouldn't be taken uncritically as a rationale for enormous financial rewards.

Similarly, analysis of pay data at UK companies highlights the lack of relationship between how the economy rewards people and the usefulness of their work to society. Regulations require the biggest companies on the UK stock market to publish the pay of the CEO as well as that of the UK employee at the 75th, median and 50th percentile point of the UK workforce (i.e. the points at which employees earn more than a quarter, half or three quarters of their colleagues).

The pay levels in financial service firms stands out a mile from the rest – at private equity firm Intermediate Capital the cut-off point for the top quarter was £375,000 in 2021, meaning that a quarter of their UK employees earned *at least* this amount.[44] At investment manager Ninety One a quarter of UK employees made at least £285,000. At hedge fund Man Group, the cut-off point was £273,000. It is worth reiterating that these are not just the pay awards made to the top executives, but to a quarter of their employees. The seemingly extraordinary pay levels are consistent with wider research showing that more people in the top 1 per cent, the top 0.1 per cent and the top 0.01 per cent by income work in financial services than in any other profession.[45]

In contrast, across the aerospace and engineering companies in the FTSE 350, the cut-off points for the top quarter of UK earners range from £43,000 to £82,000. This illustrates how people at the top in finance tend to make far more than their counterparts in other industries, even those requiring highly specialised skills, knowledge and experience.

In terms of the complexity of the work or the training and skills required, there is no obvious reason why people in financial services deserve so much more money than highly skilled manufacturing workers building cars or aircraft or high-tech industrial equipment.

Financial services industry lobbyists would argue that pay in the industry reflects market value, the price that clients seeking financial services are willing to pay, and that this in turn demonstrates the industry's value to society as a whole. But should the value dictated by the market be the only or overwhelming determinant of reward levels? This ignores many aspects that could affect what people deserve to be paid, like personal risks involved in their work, the arduousness or unpleasantness of the work, or societal value as judged by a different arbiter than a market with dubious claims to being free and functional. A cleaner or a refuse collector or a care assistant might work longer hours doing work that is much harder to endure than an investment banker (or a corporate lawyer or a tech engineer for a social media company or a management consultant or audit partner). They might face greater risks to their health. The positive outcomes that their work delivers for society are certainly a good deal more clear cut. Indeed it is very easy to find instances of highly paid financial services professionals delivering the exact opposite.

For example, the 2022 annual report of the UN Conference on Trade and Development sets out how the outsized influence of financial speculators on commodity markets distorts food and energy prices, destabilising prices and exacerbating hardship in both the developed and developing world.[46]

In 2021, the *Daily Mail* newspaper – an organ not noted for its critical views of the capitalist economic system – ran a week-long series of articles highlighting the ruinous consequences that the private equity investment model has had for a number of businesses in Britain, as wealthy investors buy up companies in debt-funded deals, pass the debt on to the companies and personally profit from selling off their assets.[47]

Practices like high frequency, short term trading of financial assets or 'short-selling' (effectively betting on companies failing by borrowing their shares, selling them and then buying them back for a lower price to return to the original lender) have also attracted major concerns from financial experts. They have dubious benefits in terms of providing additional liquidity or information for market participants. Meanwhile, they capture investment that could be used to invest in productive companies, and potentially destabilise the businesses targeted (indeed they can create an active incentive to destabilise them).[48]

Even these activities – which might merely be considered unethical – compare favourably with the financial services professionals who spend their extremely well-remunerated working lives committing literal crimes and violating regulations. The 'violation tracker' monitoring the fines and penalties issued to corporations for issues like competition offences or customer exploitation in the UK shows that the five FTSE 100 banks (Barclays, HSBC, Lloyds, NatWest and Standard Chartered) have accumulated over £2 billion in fines for 120 different offences in the UK since the tracker began keeping records in 2010.[49] In the US, four major investment banks (JP Morgan, Goldman Sachs, Citigroup and Bank of America) have been fined £171 billion for nearly 900 offences going back to 2000.[50]

The frequency of these incidents makes it hard to avoid the conclusion that the banking industry has effectively accepted that some level of malpractice or criminality is inevitable and that the resultant fines are essentially a cost of business.

Unearned rewards are not inevitable

While this does not necessarily mean that bankers and the super-rich can be dismissed as frauds, crooks and sociopaths in their entirety, the above examples demonstrate that extreme incomes and wealth are being accumulated on a major scale from activities ranging from the unethical to the illegal, with the costs being borne by wider society. When the extent to which the super-rich profit from socially useless or harmful activity is set alongside the prevalence of vast rewards for failure, the huge fortunes they accumulate as a result of other people's work and the huge advantages that they typically enjoy in life, the notion that their income and wealth levels reflect an earned outcome that is somehow fair or proportionate to their effort, productivity or socio-economic contribution becomes totally ridiculous.

The next chapter will look at policies that could address this situation and explain why a fairer, more balanced distribution of incomes and wealth is entirely feasible.

6

How to Abolish the Super-Rich

Previous chapters have argued that the outsized fortunes of the super-rich are way beyond what is necessary to incentivise or reward innovation and productivity; that we could achieve potentially massive uplifts to living standards by rebalancing their excess income and wealth; that this would lead to a more prosperous, stable, greener economy better equipped to deal with the challenges of the future; and that the super-rich do not earn or deserve their riches in either an economic or moral sense.

These are the reasons *why* we should abolish the super-rich, but what about the *how*? The purpose of this book is to draw attention to the towering levels of income and wealth captured by the super-rich, and the potential and justification for redistributing and pre-distributing these extreme concentrations, as a starting point for discussion. It is not intended to provide an exhaustive or definitive list of the policies necessary to achieve this (not least because there are multiple different measures governments could undertake that would all have a beneficial effect and different countries may choose to use different ones).

However, the argument that we need a major programme of pre-distribution and redistribution depends on convincing people that it is not just desirable but feasible. One of the key findings of the focus groups discussed in the introductory chapter to this book was that participants were deeply cynical about the possibility of government ever doing anything about the super-rich (regardless of whether or not they wanted them to).

While it's probably grounded in experience, such cynicism is actually unjustified. There are countless ways of rebalancing incomes and wealth away from the super-rich to the advantage of everybody else, supported by rigorous research and analysis and often already applied successfully in certain countries. This chapter will highlight some examples, not as a definitive manifesto for abolishing the super-rich but as a means of illustrating that it is a totally reasonable and realistic aim.

We need both redistribution and pre-distribution of incomes and wealth

The likeliest vehicle for achieving a more even balance of income and wealth is a government committed to an anti-super-rich (i.e. pro everybody else) agenda. Social movements can have an impact without waiting for political parties and governments to take a lead, but organic change in response to campaigns and engagement tends to happen in a more limited way over a longer time period than changes mandated by government policies.

While higher taxes on the super-rich are probably the policies that would most readily come to mind in this respect, they are not the only or even necessarily the most important ones. Despite being almost offensively hideous policy jargon, this book has used the terms redistribution and pre-distribution throughout in order to emphasise repeatedly that as well as taxing the super-rich we need to stop them accumulating such disproportionate income and wealth in the first place. This is borne out by figures published by the Office for National Statistics suggesting that the UK reduces income inequality (meaning inequality throughout society, not just between the super-rich and everybody else) to a slightly lesser extent than most of the more equal societies in Western Europe, but original pre-tax income inequality is much higher in the UK to begin with. For example, the figures showed the Gini coefficient in the UK falls by 44.7 per cent as a result of taxes and transfers, 1.7 percentage points less than the reduction to inequality that taxes delivered in Sweden and 4.2 less than in the Netherlands.[1] However, pre-tax income inequality in the UK was 5.5 points higher than in the Netherlands and 8.2 points higher than in Sweden.

In other words, the differences in original income accounted for a bigger proportion of the difference in inequality between the UK and these countries, than differences in how much we taxed and redistributed. It follows that in order to demonstrate the feasibility of tackling the super-rich, pre-distributive policies should be promoted as vigorously as redistributive ones.

Corporate governance reforms could get big employers spending less on their bosses and more on everybody else

One of the most obvious ways to 'pre-distribute' would be to change corporate governance regulations that currently encourage an approach to business that sees executives as the drivers of business success and returns to shareholders as the overriding priority. Changing these regulations could create a different kind of business culture, more understanding of the contribution of the wider workforce to organisational success and more focused on betterment of workers' living standards as a key business objective.

Large corporations are major generators of income and wealth, but as has already been noted, do not do so with any degree of evenness or equity. Power to influence the governance of UK and US firms resides almost exclusively with highly paid investment industry professionals. As shareholders, they can vote on strategic decisions and the appointment of board members, whereas workers have no say at all. In the UK, directors have a legal duty to act in the interests of shareholders, but only to 'have regard' for those of other stakeholders.[2]

Meanwhile, UK and US workers have almost no rights to participation in corporate governance (despite the fact that businesses are much more dependent on workers to operate than shareholders). This is in contrast with the majority of corporate governance systems across Europe, which give workers the right to representation on company boards.[3] The European Participation Index, maintained by the European Trade Union Institute, ranked the UK 26th out of 28 European countries (EU member states plus the UK) for 'democracy at work', ahead of only Latvia and Estonia.[4]

A requirement for companies to elect worker directors onto company boards, as is already the case in much of Europe, would ensure that when major employers are making decisions on budgets, and pay specifically, the workers' perspective is heard in the decision-making process. Worker directors are much more likely to emphasise decent pay and working conditions as an intrinsically important business objective rather than assume that the primary purpose of the company is simply to make profits for shareholders.

This would increase the likelihood of more balanced pay structures within the company, and a balance between pay and profits more favourable to the workers and less favourable to the wealthy investors. Worker directors can also improve operational understanding of the business, diversify the range of backgrounds and perspectives involved with decision-making processes and provide insights into employee engagement and well-being. So there is a very robust economic case for mandating them, even from a conventional business perspective.

Stronger trade unions would empower workers in pay negotiations

Enhanced levels of boardroom representation would give workers greater influence over corporate pay practices more generally, through their oversight of allocation of revenues and expenditure. These measures could also be complemented by policies to strengthen low and middle earners' bargaining power over their own pay specifically.

One of the best ways to do this would be by widening access to trade union representation. It is no coincidence that the share of total incomes captured by the top 1 per cent over the past century in the UK has fallen and then risen in almost perfect synchronisation with the increase followed by the decline in the proportion of the population who are members of a trade union.[5] Evidence from the International Labour Organization also shows that countries with higher collective bargaining coverage – where more workers jointly negotiate their pay, often via a trade union, rather than individually – tend to have lower levels of income inequality.[6] A report by the US Department of the Treasury estimates that unionised workers earn about 10–15 per cent more than non-unionised counterparts in similar roles.[7] This makes sense. Unions can speak freely and frankly to employers without fear of recrimination. They have negotiating experience and access to extensive research and data that they can draw on to strengthen their position in pay negotiations. And if necessary, they can coordinate strikes, media or social media activity or other tactics designed to exert pressure on employers.

However, it is not always easy for trade unions to organise, and in some countries it is made unnecessarily difficult. In the UK, unions do not currently have a right to access workplaces to tell workers about the benefits of union membership or key employment rights, such as the right to be consulted on major business decisions or rights to breaks and paid holidays.

It is often the lowest-paid workers in industries such as social care, hospitality, warehouse operations, security work or agriculture and food processing where awareness of rights at work and union membership are also lowest, creating a vicious cycle as conditions become more exploitative and fall further behind those for better-paid work. Employers are also currently only required to commit to a recognition agreement with a union, covering issues like working conditions and, critically, the right to a collective bargaining process, if at least 10 per cent of the workforce request it.

In traditional workplaces where, for example, the same workers would stand next to each other every day on a factory production line, support for collective bargaining was rather easier to secure than in much of the modern economy where atomised workforces are increasingly common (for example, where many different languages are spoken, where staff turnover is high or shift patterns varied). This is especially the case if starting from scratch in an organisation with a limited union presence. Low-paid workers are often doing low-paid work as a result of limited options, so are sometimes understandably wary of undertaking an activity such as union participation that they fear might be perceived negatively by management and threaten their job security.

In the US, there is similarly a lack of guaranteed access, and employers frequently go to extreme lengths to influence employee votes on unionisation, with examples cited by academic experts on industrial relations including plastering the walls with anti-union leaflets, playing anti-union videos on loop and forcing employees to attend anti-union presentations.[8] Pro-union employees are obviously unable to use such tactics, rendering the votes on whether to unionise as fair and democratic as the 'elections' in North Korea or Saddam Hussein's Iraq. Employees who have agitated for union recognition have also been subject to sudden changes in shift patterns, harassment by management and spurious dismissals.

Fortunately, there are a number of proposals for ways in which it can be made easier for unions to fulfil the vital role they play in a democratic, free market economy, and for workers to make a free, informed choice about the benefits of union membership.

For example, in New Zealand, trade unions have a guaranteed right of reasonable access to workplaces where they think work relevant to the objectives of the union is being carried out.[9] This could be supplemented by a requirement on employers to inform any new employees of relevant unions in their industry.

In the US, pro-union policymakers have proposed laws that would ban companies from interfering with votes on unionisation and introduce much harsher penalties for mistreatment of pro-union employees.[10]

In the UK, the union movement has called for sectoral 'fair pay agreements', beginning with industries like social care or catering and hospitality, where poor pay and working conditions are particularly prevalent.[11] These agreements could bring together employers, unions and independent experts to agree pay levels, conditions and other employment standards across the sector. While the agreements would mostly concentrate on ensuring adequate pay for low-earning workers – which in itself would be an indirect form of pre-distribution of the income and wealth of the super-rich – they could also look at pay gaps between the lowest- and highest-paid workers in the sector, putting a more direct limit on the ability of executives to profit from poverty pay.

Measures like these, facilitating a much stronger trade union presence at major employers, would help to resist and reverse the increase in the share of total incomes that the top 1 per cent have captured at the expense of the other 99 per cent as union representation declined.

Worker ownership and profit-sharing mechanisms channel corporate wealth to the people who create it

As a complement or alternative to indirect measures like worker representation on boards or stronger trade unions that would facilitate pre-distribution of the income and wealth of the super-rich, there are also ways simply to mandate pre-distribution directly, through worker share ownership and profit-sharing schemes, for example.

In the UK, there are currently very few businesses where workers own a significant share of the company and where the profits directly accrue to the people whose time and effort ultimately creates them, despite some high-profile examples like John Lewis or Richer Sounds. In 2016 (the most recent year for which data is available) there were only 35 companies out of 600 listed on the UK stock market where more than 10 per cent of shares were held by employees (despite the fact that at that date these companies had outperformed the wider index by 130 per cent over the previous ten years). Just 20 UK companies with more than 1,000 employees are more than 25 per cent employee-owned.[12] Similarly, in the US employee-owned companies (defined as being more than 30 per cent employee-owned) account for fewer than 2 per cent of total employment.[13]

This means that there is great potential to address extreme concentrations of income and wealth, through the expansion of worker ownership, thereby redirecting the mega profits of big corporations away from the super-rich and into the pockets of those who need and deserve them more.

Models for how to do this already exist. The Commonwealth think tank has developed a proposal (adding detail to a 2019 Labour Party election manifesto commitment) that would require companies with over 250 employees to pay up to 10 per cent of dividend payments linked to UK economic activity to an 'inclusive ownership fund' on behalf of their UK workforce. Commonwealth estimate that by 2029, this would generate £6 billion annually for workers at these companies – income that would have otherwise have gone to mainly wealthy investors.[14]

Similarly, in France, companies with more than 50 employees recording total profits of more than 5 per cent of the value of the company are compelled to share an agreed proportion of their profits with their employees (if the company and the employees fail to come to an agreement on how the proportion will be calculated, the state imposes a calculation).[15]

While not a form of ownership, profit-sharing mechanisms have very similar effects in terms of guaranteeing workers a proportion of profits that would otherwise accrue to investors. A research paper published in 2023 found that the French mechanism had increased the incomes of low-earning workers at the affected companies without having any negative impact on investment of productivity.[16] Wider international adoption of mechanisms to promote worker ownership and profit-sharing would be likely to replicate this effect.

A maximum wage would raise low earners' pay rises along with top bosses'

As well as ensuring workers get a fair share of the profits their company generates, governments could set rules guaranteeing a fair division of the total expenditure on pay. Just as we have a statutory minimum wage in the UK, to ensure that the lowest-paid workers are not exploited by their employers, we could also have a statutory maximum to address the absurd pay gaps between top earners and the majority of their colleagues.

There is a case for this based on fairness and proportionality. The most senior, highly paid staff in an organisation tend to have strongest relationships with the board members or executive team. They have the most extensive professional networks (increasing their potential to attract work elsewhere). And they fill roles with the most influence over the organisation, thereby causing greater upheaval if they leave. This means that they are able to extract higher pay than they necessarily merit, and regulatory intervention to prevent them doing so would ensure fairer, more proportionate outcomes.

Given employers' susceptibility to the myth of the unique abilities of the superstar executive described in previous chapters, there is also a related business case. For individuals with experience or skillsets deemed to be rarer and of higher value, employers are under greater pressure to raise their pay to attract or retain their services. Rival firms are then compelled to do likewise, particularly if there is perceived to be a difference in the capability of the limited number of people with this experience or skillset. Firms will feel that if they pay less than their rivals, they are likely to have to appoint a less capable candidate. Thus, all firms are incentivised to push pay upwards and when everybody does the same thing, none are in a better position to attract and retain senior staff.

A cap on top earnings would address this problem, saving companies money that could potentially be used to pay the rest of the workforce more. The cap could be expressed as a fixed amount, but might work better as a multiple of the pay of the lowest-paid worker (for example 10 or 20 times) creating an incentive for executives to raise the pay of the wider work-force. It would cover all forms of payment received in the year, including bonuses and share awards.

There is no international precedent for a maximum wage, but Second World War-era US President Roosevelt proposed a 100 per cent tax on high incomes during the war, on the basis that it was inefficient for the country's much-needed resources to accrue to people who already had more than enough.[17] This logic ought to be just as applicable outside of war time, in soci-eties where a large proportion of the population suffers from insufficient levels of income. The management expert Peter Drucker (commenting in 1998) and John Pierpoint Morgan (in the early twentieth century), the founder of the JP Morgan bank, also both advocated for caps of 20 to 1, to limit the pay of the highest earners.[18] There are already some employers that apply a cap voluntarily – at the John Lewis retail chain in the UK, the CEO cannot claim more than 75 times average pay, which is admittedly not a huge sacrifice in the name of economic equality, but it does effectively guarantee that their CEO is paid substantially less than the top managers of almost every comparably sized UK retailer.[19] Much more meaningful ratios are commonplace in the charity sector; at Christian Aid, for example, the ratio is set at 4:1.[20]

More recently there have been less drastic versions of essentially the same idea. San Francisco voters voted for an additional 1 per cent corporation tax to be added to the tax bill for companies whose CEOs were paid more than 100 times their lowest-paid worker.[21] Similarly, it has been proposed that pay above a certain threshold could be made non-tax-deductible, meaning excessive top pay would still be permitted, but more expensive and thus disincentivised.

With some companies spending in excess of £20 million on one or two executives alone, a cap resulting in top pay levels in the low hundreds of thousands would save companies vast sums of money that could be used to support pay increases for other workers (or invested in the business to the benefit of all). If companies are unable to recruit capable leaders for this amount of money, they should question their own recruitment and training policies, and ask why people won't work for them in theoretically attractive and prestigious roles, unless they are paid millions of pounds.

While a maximum wage might seem radical to business elites and policymakers, we should perhaps ask what might appear stranger and more extreme to an intelligent life form landing on earth and wanting to learn about the organisation of life on the planet – a system that limited the pay of top earners to perhaps 20 times their lowest- or median-earning colleague, or one where people earn over 100 times others working alongside them in the same organisation, with all the resultant discrepancies in living standards that this entails?

Taxes on the super-rich would bring widespread benefits for everybody else

Very many people work in large businesses – roughly 11 million in the UK – so pre-distributive measures affecting these companies would play a massive role in transferring income and wealth from the super-rich investors that own them and the executives that run them to the lower and middle earners that work for them, raising living standards for vast numbers of people in the process.

However, this 11 million only accounts for about one sixth of the UK population. Even assuming that many of them will have partners, children and other family members who would also see their household incomes rise, it still leaves a lot of people not benefiting.

This is why redistribution through taxes would also play a role in tackling the problem of the super-rich and raising living standards for households beyond those that work for large and profitable employers.

Increasing tax revenues could enable pay rises for millions of public sector workers, including National Health Service staff, teachers, local government workers and the police. Higher tax revenues would also increase the funding available for climate change mitigation, health and social care, education, public safety, social security, policing, public transport, housing and the justice system. This funding would help to address many of the most severe crises in British society and would massively improve the quality of public services and thus the living standards of the wider population.

Governments could gather far more tax revenue from the super-rich for these purposes than is currently the case (without really compromising their super-rich status). And there are already a number of detailed proposals on how we might begin to tax very high levels of income and wealth more effectively, backed up by academic research.

For example, the UK's 2020 Wealth Tax Commission, involving academics from the LSE Inequalities Institute and the CAGE Research Centre at Warwick University, examines the scope for greater taxation of extreme wealth. The Commission's tax simulator allows researchers to compare the impact of different levels of wealth taxation and how they might apply in different scenarios. A tax rate of 2 per cent on wealth levels over £5 million would raise between £15 billion and £24 billion, depending on the levels of avoidance and whether or not rich list entrants living overseas are included. Annual administrative costs would amount to £12 million, and the tax would be paid in its entirety by individuals comfortably inside the wealthiest 1 per cent.[22]

A minority of people in this wealth bracket might have insufficient liquidity to cover the cost of the tax – for example, business owners whose business might have a high value based on its future potential but not yet generating the profits to cover the wealth tax. However, the overwhelming majority of people with super-rich levels of wealth would expect to generate significant returns from that wealth – such as profits from businesses they own, or rental income from properties. The possibility to defer payments could be integrated into the tax structure for the small proportion who might suffer from liquidity issues. Similarly, provisions could be made for tax contributions to be paid in shares rather than cash, which would then be sold on by the government, averting any potential for disputes over valuation.

Research from the Commission also notes the potential to generate substantial additional revenue for public services from the super-rich through reform of existing taxes. For example, capital gains (the profits made from the sale of assets, such as company shares or an investment property) are taxed at a lower rate than income from work. This favours the rich, who are far more likely to own properties, businesses or a share portfolio. Increasing capital gains tax to the same rate as income tax would generate about £16 billion for public services.[23] The research estimated that more than half of total income from capital gains accrues to just 5,000 people, less than 0.001 per cent of the population. So the bulk of this £16 billion could be gathered from a group of millionaires and billionaires small enough to fit in the Royal Albert Hall (and at a tax rate of 40 per cent it would amount to less than half their capital gains for the year).

Similarly, National Insurance contributions (NICs) are again only paid on income from work, while investment income accruing to owners of wealth such as landlords and investors is unaffected. NICs are also currently paid at a reduced rate on earnings over £50,000, while those of state pension age and above don't pay any NICs, regardless of their income. Closing these loopholes would raise about £15 billion, even if the tax rate were cut by 1.25 per cent to compensate for the broadening of the number of people affected.[24] Over half of this revenue would come from those with incomes of over £100,000 and nearly a fifth from the circa 0.1 per cent of the population making over £500,000. So while around a tenth of the revenue would come from those with an income of under £35,000, this would be overwhelmingly a tax on the super-rich.

Together, these measures would generate tens of billions of pounds worth of funding for the UK, to support public services and investment in the economy, from what are actually quite undramatic changes to taxation that the super-rich could easily afford.

To differing degrees and in different ways, the same is true in most other economies. In the US, for example, economists at Berkeley University have previously estimated that a wealth tax at a rate of 2 per cent on fortunes of over $50 million and 3 per cent on those over $1 billion would raise around $3 trillion over a ten-year period from 2023.[25] The economists also outline why some of the difficulties implementing and administering a wealth tax are exaggerated. While valuing wealth held in assets like fine artworks or precious jewellery is challenging, 70 per cent of the wealth of the top 0.1 per cent in the US is held in publicly listed companies whose market value is publicly available, while most of the remaining 30 per cent is held in private companies – establishing a fair value for these companies is the kind of thing financial analysts do every day and should be a straightforward task for a well-resourced Inland Revenue Service or international equivalent.

At global level, an open letter published ahead of the G20 summit in India in 2023 and signed by economists, political representatives and millionaires themselves from across all six continents, called for the leaders of the world's most powerful economies to take action to enact a new international tax regime that would lead to more effective and higher taxation of the super-rich. This demonstrates the common interest in rebalancing extreme concentrations of income and wealth, and highlights the weaknesses of the argument that countries that take action to strengthen their public services will face negative economic consequences for doing so. The potential to close gaping inequalities, improve public services and raise levels of income and wealth and living standards by tackling the problem of the super-rich is shared the world over. As discussed in chapter 4, there are multiple precedents for countries agreeing common approaches or solutions to issues that transcend national borders, and enacting changes that benefit each of their populations.

The feasibility of tackling the problem of the super-rich depends on our will to do it

While, as has been repeatedly emphasised, the list of policies discussed in this chapter is not fully exhaustive, it highlights how there are plenty of mechanisms that governments could commit to implementing as part of this process. Tackling the problem of the super-rich is not some kind of interesting but unfeasible objective like time travel or the secret of perpetual motion – it is something we could get started on tomorrow.

Most of the defences of the prevailing extreme imbalances of income and wealth are not positive arguments exalting the contribution of the super-rich, how hard they work or what a generous, compassionate and public-spirited group of people they are, because that would immediately and correctly be dismissed and ridiculed. The case against doing anything about the super-rich relies on impossible-ism and a 'can't do' attitude that claims it is either economically or politically not feasible.

Ultimately, the validity of this argument comes down to how much public appetite there is for the rebalancing of income and wealth, the extent to which people support the general principle of a reasonably fair/equal society and the belief that policies such as those mentioned would raise living standards.

When a particular narrative takes hold in public consciousness and is widely understood and supported, the policies tend to follow. The previously cited examples about progress on environmental issues or corporation tax – painstakingly achieved over years of hard work, taking them from relatively fringe issues to global priorities – illustrate this point. One could also look at the creation of welfare states and expansion of public services in the twentieth century as case studies of major political and economic changes that ultimately came about because inequality and the condition of the working classes became increasingly salient politically to the point that politicians who advocated the provision of a much stronger social security safer net, public housing or the National Health Service were able to win elections.

If there was widespread agreement – particularly across different national populations – that the super-rich do not merit their extreme riches and that pre-distributing or redistributing their incomes and wealth should be an urgent and priority objective for governments, policies and action would swiftly follow.

The concluding chapter of this book will argue that with living standards stagnating, public services collapsing and the hoarding of incomes and wealth by the super-rich creating an intolerable obstacle to social progress, the potential to create this kind of consensual agreement across the political spectrum, is high.

Conclusion

Servility to the super-rich has done little for wider living standards

When a Labour MP opined in a BBC radio interview ahead of the 2019 UK general election that billionaires should not exist, the presenter was incredulous and later tweeted that it was an 'extraordinary' comment.[1] The interview was followed up by days of mostly critical discussion in the press.

It's surprising that the suggestion that, in an ideal world, the world's richest people should try and struggle by with wealth of just £999 million pounds, something like 200 times the average national lottery jackpot, prompts such derision.[2] Particularly when the growing number of billionaires appear to be contributing very little to wider prosperity.

Research by the Resolution Foundation think tank suggests that in the UK average wages adjusted for inflation will not reach 2008 levels until 2027, meaning pay has stagnated for nearly two decades.[3] Similarly, data from the World Bank show that between 2008 and 2022 on a per capita basis, adjusted for inflation and differences in the cost of living, the UK economy grew by just 7 per cent, compared to 12 per cent in Germany and 17 per cent in the US.[4]

The idea that this dreadful record has come about as a result of being too focused on distribution at the expense of growth is far fetched. The UK is one of the most unequal high-income countries in the world and the Gini coefficient of income distribution hasn't really changed over the last decade. The

OECD ranks the UK 8th most unequal out of 40 major economies, more unequal than every EU country except Bulgaria.[5] The number of UK billionaires recorded by the Sunday Times Rich List since 2008 has increased from 75 to 171.

If we really have been obsessed with distribution, it has not been a productive obsession.

In reality, the UK is widely considered to be relatively speaking a more small-state, laissez-faire economy compared to other high-income countries. The UK government spends less as a proportion of GDP than almost any other Western European country, according to the IMF.[6] 'Social spending', that is, expenditure on social housing and social security payments, for example, is also lower as a proportion of government expenditure.[7] This is a pretty good proxy for how bothered a country is about inequality and the distribution of incomes and wealth, and the UK does not register as being overly concerned. The same can be said, even more emphatically, of America. The US government spends even less as a proportion of GDP, and even less of this goes on social spending on poorer and disadvantaged households.

A major programme of redistribution and pre-distribution is realistic and pragmatic

The problems of weak growth, stagnating living standards, and high inequality demand a more meaningful response than that provided by the politicians cited in the introduction of this book prattling on about the need to grow pies and cakes.

It would, of course, be great if we could reduce inequality by just making the poorest people in society as rich as the richest ones. Similarly, in an ideal world, geographic economic differences, the focus of Boris Johnson's ill-fated 'levelling up' agenda in the UK, would be addressed by making the less prosperous regions grow to the level of the most dynamic without requiring subsidies from one to the other. Going back further, Robin Hood might have proven a less divisive figure in medieval Nottingham had he concentrated on giving to the poor, rather than fuelling the politics of envy by robbing the rich as well.

Unfortunately, the only place that politicians who encourage this kind of thinking as an actual approach to government are likely to be growing pies is in the sky. If it was that easy for everybody to have more without anybody else having less, it would probably already be happening on a much greater scale (and indeed quite a lot of historical strife, which very commonly has its roots in competition for finite resources, would have been avoided). While advocates of redistribution or pre-distribution are often accused of being simplistic or unrealistic, proponents of the master plan to solve inequality and raise living standards by making all the poor people as rich as the rich ones probably aren't in a position to lecture anyone on proposals that are vacuous, utopian and insubstantial. Twenty-first-century societies do not have infinite resources, and the necessary 'tough choices' so venerated in modern politics must include the choice to take on very wealthy and powerful individuals and corporations to ensure that their excessive riches are put towards a more socially useful purpose.

That is not to say that we should give up on trying to generate economic growth altogether. Instead, it should be noted that, as discussed in chapter 3 of this book, there is a lot of evidence that addressing the problem of the super-rich would boost overall growth, rather than hinder it. At the same time, growth will be difficult to achieve and it will not have the desired impact on living standards unless accompanied by more significant redistribution and pre-distribution.

Highlighting the challenges of delivering more significant growth as part of the case for action on the problem of the super-rich risks falsely conflating a more even balance of income and wealth with a smaller economy. But the fact that growth and its positive impact on wider living standards cannot be easily guaranteed is worth addressing.

First, there is considerable disagreement, even among economists and other experts, about how to generate growth – and some of the measures most widely agreed to do so in the UK, like increasing immigration or relaxing planning regulations, have proved politically contentious to put it mildly. Similarly, as demographic change shrinks the working-age proportion of the population and climate change puts further pressure on the price of food, energy and other vital commodities, the much-desired growth of pie or cake may prove elusive. In which case, redistribution or pre-distribution would be an effective way to do more with the same resources, making life better for those in the middle and at the bottom. Those at the top would remain comparatively rich (albeit slightly less so than was previously the case).

Second, even if we do successfully stimulate much more substantial levels of economic growth than have been achieved in recent years, this will have minimal impact on the living standards of the people who need it most unless we address the way the proceeds of growth are currently distributed. The World Inequality Database suggests that the bottom 50 per cent of the UK income distribution receive around 20 per cent of total pre-tax incomes.[8] In other words, for every £1 of income going to people in Britain, the poorest half of the population get 20p. So 80 per cent of any income growth is going to bypass the people with the lowest incomes if we don't change the balance of distribution.

In America, where inequality is even more pronounced, the bottom 50 per cent of the population take just 14 per cent of total incomes. This is perhaps why, despite a better recent record on economic growth in the US, the problems discussed in the introduction to this book such as falling life expectancy and rising 'deaths of despair' (from drugs, alcohol or suicide) continue to afflict the country to a worse extent than almost any other in the developed world.[9]

Addressing extreme concentrations of income and wealth is the real centrism

It would be supremely naïve not to recognise that these arguments will resonate most with people on the political left and that this book will mainly have a left-wing audience. Nonetheless, one of the frequent observations writing it was that surely some of the arguments might appeal to those in the centre and on the right.

The contrast between the future funding needs of public services and infrastructure, and the multiple cost of living challenges facing so many middle and low earners on the one hand with the extraordinary riches of the super-rich on the other, ought to make any pragmatic centrist at least curious about the possibility of using the latter to address the former.

While critics on the libertarian right would probably recoil from measures designed to raise taxes or regulate businesses, there are also conservatives who might see the extreme riches hoarded by the super-rich as an affront to values traditionally cherished on the right like personal responsibility and patriotism. The super-rich, and the companies that they manage and invest in, could contribute much more to their country in terms of paying taxes and paying their employees more fairly.

The fact that they don't ought to irritate 'one nation' Tories and their international equivalents as much as it does the left.

It should also be noted that it would be easier to lower taxes for the majority of the people if they were higher on the super-rich. Given factors like climate change and ageing populations, many people might question the wisdom of a tax-cutting agenda, but it does become more realistic to reduce the tax burden on those in the middle and at the bottom (to whom it would actually make a difference) by increasing them on those at the very top.

Away from economic policy there are many other things – like stopping immigration, taking a harder line on law and order, or restarting the hundred years war – that right-wing people would presumably like and that aren't incompatible with a less supine approach to the super-rich. Indeed, the capacity of border controls, the police, the prison service and the military would all be much stronger in the event of higher taxes on the rich providing them with more resources.

That is not to say that any of these policies would be a good idea. The point is that there is a basis to build a consensus on the need to tackle the problem of the super-rich across people who hold diverse views on many other matters. No doubt energetic debate and disagreement on such issues would continue. It's just that those debates would take place in a society where public services are better funded, life chances are less affected by hugely excessive differences in income and wealth, and people are rewarded more proportionately to the contribution that they make and the work that they do.

It is time to abolish the super-rich

Part of the impetus to write this book came from the fact that in the current economic context, the case for a more even distribution of income and wealth seemed like the most basic common sense. We could make a huge difference to living standards through a more balanced distribution, while the super-rich would remain very well incentivised and rewarded for whatever success they have achieved. Across multiple economies, the share of income, wealth, or both captured by the super-rich, and the extent of the gap between those at the top and everybody else, would have caused absolute horror 40, 30 or even 20 years ago but as a result of incremental increases it is now widely assumed to be the natural order of things.

Yet despite the difference the enormous and actually existing incomes and wealth accruing to a few very rich people could make to the wider population if it was distributed more evenly, anyone pointing this out is generally treated as a fantasist or an extremist. Meanwhile promising to simply make everyone rich with hitherto non-existent wealth is heralded as the hallmark of sober and serious policymaking.

The book is intended to help get a debate going that moves the issue of the super-rich more into the political mainstream and encourages a wider recognition that the pre-distribution and redistribution of their income and wealth are fundamental to addressing the biggest challenges we face as a society.

Anyone who looks pragmatically at the issue of how to deliver meaningful reductions to poverty and improvements to the living standards of huge numbers of people ought to recognise that the fortunes of the super-rich provide a vast and readily available resource that could contribute to these purposes were it not concentrated so inefficiently. Indeed, it will be impossible achieve our full potential to build a fairer, happier, more prosperous society without a major rebalancing of incomes and wealth. This ought not to be a question of partisan ideology – the logic, feasibility and urgent importance of the issue are clear. It is time to abolish the super-rich.

Notes

Introduction

1. This saying is often attributed to Winston Churchill, but is included on a list of famous quotes he never actually said by the Hillsdale College Churchill Project; Hillsdale College, All the 'quotes' Churchill never said (3: Lies to sex), 23 November 2018, https://richardlangworth.com/quotes-churchill-never-said-3 (accessed 7 March 2023).
2. Trades Union Congress, UK workers will miss out on £3,600 in pay this year as a result of wages not keeping pace with the OECD, 10 July 2023, www.tuc.org.uk/news/uk-workers-will-miss-out-ps3600-pay-year-result-wages-not-keeping-pace-oecd (accessed 10 July 2023).
3. Trussell Trust, End of year stats, [April] 2023, www.trusselltrust.org/news-and-blog/latest-stats/end-year-stats/ (accessed 1 July 2023).
4. *Which?* One in seven skipping meals due to rising cost of living, Which? finds, 7 March 2023, https://press.which.co.uk/whichpressreleases/one-in-seven-skipping-meals-due-to-rising-cost-of-living-which-finds/ (accessed 1 July 2023).
5. Full Fact, The overall NHS waiting list continues to rise, 14 June 2023, https://fullfact.org/health/rishi-sunak-cutting-waiting-lists/ (accessed 1 July 2023).
6. King's Fund, *How Does the NHS Compare to the Health Care Systems of Other Countries?*, 2023, www.kingsfund.org.uk/sites/default/files/2023-06/How_NHS_compare_2023.pdf (accessed 1 July 2023).
7. World Inequality Database, Income and wealth inequality, United Kingdom, 1820–2021, 2023, https://wid.world/country/united-kingdom/ (accessed 1 July 2023).
8. *Sunday Times*, The Sunday Times Rich List 2023, www.thetimes.co.uk/sunday-times-rich-list (accessed 1 July 2023).
9. Institute for Policy Studies, *Billionaire Enabler States: How the US States Captured by the Trust Industry Help the World's Wealthy Hide their Fortunes*, September 2022, https://ips-dc.org/wp-content/uploads/2022/09/IPS-Billionaire-Enabler-States.pdf (accessed 17 July 2023).
10. Harvard University, Why life expectancy in the US is falling, 20 October 2022, www.health.harvard.edu/blog/why-life-expectancy-in-the-us-is-

falling-202210202835#:~:text=With%20rare%20exceptions%2C%20
life%20expectancy,year%20span%20since%20the%201920s (accessed
17 July 2023).

11. Trust for America's Health, Pain in the nation 2023: U.S. death rate due
to alcohol, drugs, and suicide increased by 11 percent in 2021, 24 May
2023, www.tfah.org/report-details/pain-in-the-nation-2023/ (accessed
July 10 2023).

12. Center for Poverty & Inequality Research, University of California,
Davis, What is deep poverty?, 2022, https://poverty.ucdavis.edu/faq/
what-deep-poverty#:~:text=Data%20on%20those%20with%20
incomes,in%20deep%20poverty%20in%202021. (accessed 18 September 2023).

13. Kaiser Family Foundation, Key facts about the uninsured population,
19 December 2022, www.kff.org/uninsured/issue-brief/key-
facts-about-the-uninsured-population/ (accessed 17 July 2023). Figures
are for non-elderly Americans.

14. *Daily Mail*, Liz Truss: For too long politicians have fought over how to
slice up the economic pie. My mission is to make it much bigger, 24
September 2022, www.dailymail.co.uk/debate/article-11246335/LIZ-
TRUSS-long-politicians-fought-slice-economic-pie.html (accessed 7
March 2023).

15. Twitter, For decades we have focused on how we divide the pie and not
enough on growing it, 23 September 2022, https://twitter.com/Kemi
Badenoch/status/1573322584984363009 (accessed 7 March 2023) and
Sunday Times, It may look like heartless Conservatism, but trying to
spur growth is morally right, 18 September 2022, www.thetimes.co.uk/
article/it-may-look-like-heartless-conservatism-but-trying-to-spur-
growth-is-morally-right-fnxpctxnv (accessed 7 March 2023).

16. See https://twitter.com/grantshapps/status/514425573477982209, 23
September 2014.

17. *Sunday Times*, It may look like heartless conservatism but trying to
spur growth is morally right, 18 September 2022, www.thetimes.co.uk/
article/it-may-look-like-heartless-conservatism-but-trying-to-spur-
growth-is-morally-right-fnxpctxnv (accessed 7 March 2023).

18. See for example, BBC, Levelling up: Boris Johnson promises more
powers for local leaders, 15 July 2021, www.bbc.co.uk/news/uk-politics-
57844084 (accessed 7 March 2023).

19. *The Times*, Rachel Reeves for first female chancellor? George Osborne
thinks so, 7 January 2023, www.thetimes.co.uk/article/rachel-reeves-
labour-female-chancellor-keir-starmer-vkd2nqx69?t=ie (accessed 7
March 2023).

20. *Sunday Times*, Starmer must make aspiration his message, 20 December 2022, www.thetimes.co.uk/article/starmer-must-make-aspiration-his-message-lxccpgmlj (accessed 7 March 2023).

21. *Independent*, Union boss piles pressure on Labour after Reeves rules out wealth tax, 7 September 2023, www.independent.co.uk/news/uk/politics/wealth-tax-tuc-reeves-sunak-labour-b2406601.html (accessed 9 September 2023).

22. See for example comments from Democrat fundraiser Charles Myers in *Daily Mail*, Biden's raid on the richest 500,000 taxpayers: Republicans says president will increase unemployment and cut investment by raising the top income rate to 39 per cent and almost doubling capital gains, 2023, www.dailymail.co.uk/news/article-9504417/Republicans-say-presidents-tax-hikes-wealthiest-0-3-increase-unemployment.html (accessed 20 July 2023) or business leader Kevin O'Leary on YouTube: Biden's billionaire minimum income tax proposal is 'un-American,' says Kevin O'Leary, 2022, www.youtube.com/watch?v=fFXJfRTtEhQ (accessed 20 July 2023) (accessed 20 July 2023).

23. CNBC, Biden's billionaire tax is 'dead on arrival' in Congress, top Wall Street backers and Democratic strategists say, 2023, www.cnbc.com/2023/02/09/joe-bidens-billionaire-tax-is-dead-on-arrival.html (accessed 19 July 23).

24. *Guardian*, 'America v socialism': Conservatives rage against the left and plot new red scare, 1 March 2020, www.theguardian.com/us-news/2020/mar/01/trump-conservatives-socialism-bernie-sanders-politics (accessed 20 July 2023).

25. *Time*, What to know about Trump's vow to keep 'Communists' and 'Marxists' out of the U.S., June 2023, https://time.com/6290849/trump-commnunists-marxists-immigration-proposal-explainer/ (accessed 20 July 2023).

26. World Inequality Database, Income and wealth inequality, USA, 1820–2021, 2023, https://wid.world/country/usa/ (accessed 20 July 2023).

27. See for example, *Guardian*, Cap excessive pay to tackle UK jobs crisis and inequality, urges thinktank, 8 October 2020, www.theguardian.com/inequality/2020/oct/08/cap-excessive-pay-to-tackle-uk-jobs-crisis-and-inequality-urges-thinktank, or YouGov, Are taxes on the rich too high or low in Britain?, 2023, https://yougov.co.uk/topics/politics/trackers/are-taxes-on-the-rich-too-high-or-low-in-britain (accessed 8 March 2023).

28. See for example polling from YouGov showing that 63 per cent of voters did not think Labour's economic policies were feasible; YouGov, In their own words: Why voters abandoned Labour, 23 December 2019, https://yougov.co.uk/topics/politics/articles-reports/2019/12/23/

their-own-words-why-voters-abandoned-labour (accessed 6 March 2023).

29. Edelman Trust Barometer 2023, p. 46, www.edelman.co.uk/sites/g/files/aatuss301/files/2023-03/UK%20Trust%202023%20Website.pdf (accessed 30 September 2023).

30. Pew Research Centre, The casualties: Faith in hard work and capitalism, 12 July 2012, www.pewresearch.org/global/2012/07/12/chapter-4-the-casualties-faith-in-hard-work-and-capitalism/ (accessed 8 March 2023).

31. Wiley Online Library, Attitudes to wealth in seven countries: The Social Envy Coefficient and the Rich Sentiment Index, 21 June 2021, https://onlinelibrary.wiley.com/doi/full/10.1111/ecaf.12468 (accessed 8 March 2023).

32. Trust for London, *Living on Different Incomes in London: Can Public Consensus Identify a 'Riches Line'?*, February 2020, https://trustforlondon.fra1.cdn.digitaloceanspaces.com/media/documents/Living_on_Different_Incomes_in_London_Feb_2020.pdf (accessed 1 March 2023).

33. Tax Justice UK, *What's Wealth Got to Do with It? Attitudes on Public Spending, Wealth and Tax*, 2020, www.taxjustice.uk/uploads/1/0/0/3/100363766/whats_wealth_got_to_do_with_it_.pdf (accessed 13 March 2023).

1 More than Enough

1. *Guardian*, How much money makes you happy? We ask an expert, 28 October 2022, www.theguardian.com/lifeandstyle/2022/oct/28/how-much-money-makes-you-happy-we-ask-an-expert (accessed 10 July 2023).

2. Tax Justice UK, *What's Wealth Got to Do with It? Attitudes on Public Spending, Wealth and Tax*, 2020, www.taxjustice.uk/uploads/1/0/0/3/100363766/whats_wealth_got_to_do_with_it_.pdf (accessed 13 March 2023).

3. HM Revenue and Customs, Percentile points from 1 to 99 for total income before and after tax, www.gov.uk/government/statistics/percentile-points-from-1-to-99-for-total-income-before-and-after-tax#full-publication-update-history (accessed 10 March 2023). These figures are for the top 1 per cent of income tax payers – as around 40 per cent of the adult population, mainly low earners, didn't pay income tax, the thresholds for the top 1 per cent of all adults are likely to be slightly above the figures for the 2 per cent of income tax payers – respectively £125,000 pre-tax and £84,700 post-tax.

4. Office for National Statistics, Household total wealth in Great Britain: April 2018 to March 2020, 7 January 2022, www.ons.gov.uk/people populationandcommunity/personalandhouseholdfinances/income andwealth/bulletins/totalwealthingreatbritain/april2018tomarch2020 (accessed 20 September 2022).

5. DQYDJ, Income percentile calculator for the United States, 2022, https://dqydj.com/income-percentile-calculator/ (accessed 20 July 2023) and Average, median, top 1%, and all United States net worth percentiles, 2022, https://dqydj.com/average-median-top-net-worth-percentiles/ (accessed 20 July 2023).

6. The American distribution for wealth includes households with negative wealth as a result of their debts, whereas the UK adjusts for this, meaning that the differences between the 1 per cent to median wealth levels are less spectacular than these headline figures suggest.

7. Office for National Statistics, Family spending workbook 1: Detailed expenditure and trends, Table 3.1E, 2022, www.ons.gov.uk/people populationandcommunity/personalandhouseholdfinances/ expenditure/datasets/familyspendingworkbook1detailedexpenditure andtrends (accessed 4 October 2022). The data is based on weekly expenditure, with income tax and National Insurance payments not included, multiplied by 52 to estimate annual spending.

8. Figures for typical private school fees at a day school of just under £15,000 per year are taken from Think Student, How much does private school cost in the UK? – Guide for 2022, 27 January 2022, https://thinkstudent.co.uk/how-much-does-private-school-cost/ (accessed 4 October 2022). Figures for an all-inclusive seven-night stay in the Maldives, including all flight and accommodation costs of £7,000, taken from a search at Destination2.co.uk, www.destination2.co.uk/ (accessed 4 October 2022). Figures for a new BMW or Mercedes car are based on a £10,000 deposit and monthly repayment costs of £650–£700 for a 48-month agreement with the option to purchase or return the car at the end of the agreement, www.bmw.co.uk/en/index.html and https://shop.mercedes-benz.co.uk/new?gclid=CjwKCAjws--ZBhAXEiwAv-RNL6ryliN-DUjtOHCokN-3Ia233fF-stTNlLQ6ZkOqR n3OG49kpzOWaBoCq48QAvD_BwE (accessed 4 October 2022).

9. James Corden's appearance fee taken from Markmeets breaking news site and digital media agency, How much to book a celeb for 1 hour for an event?, 2022, https://markmeets.com/entertainment/celebrity-appearance-fees-revealed-just-how-much-can-stars-make/ (accessed 11 October 2022). Drug prices estimated from Drugwise, How much do drugs cost?, 2016, www.drugwise.org.uk/how-much-do-drugs-cost/ (accessed 9 September 2023) and uprated for inflation.

10. Office for National Statistics (ONS), Household total wealth in Great Britain: April 2018 to March 2020, 7 January 2022, www.ons.gov.uk/peoplepopulationandcommunity/personalandhouseholdfinances/incomeandwealth/bulletins/totalwealthingreatbritain/april2018tomarch2020 (accessed 20 September 2022). The ONS data includes breakdown of median wealth for households in the top 1%, with 46 per cent being concentrated in pensions wealth, 30 per cent property, 18 per cent financial wealth and 6 per cent physical wealth.

11. *Guardian*, Rationale behind abolition of 45p tax rate reflects failed ideology, 29 September 2022, www.theguardian.com/business/2022/sep/29/rationale-behind-abolition-of-45p-tax-rate-reflects-failed-ideology (accessed 6 March 2023).

12. *Guardian*, Rationale behind abolition of 45p tax rate reflects failed ideology, 29 September 2022, www.theguardian.com/business/2022/sep/29/rationale-behind-abolition-of-45p-tax-rate-reflects-failed-ideology (accessed 6 March 2023).

13. High Pay Centre, FTSE 100 CEOs get half a million pound pay rise, 21 August 2023, https://highpaycentre.org/ftse-100-ceos-get-half-a-million-pound-pay-rise/ (accessed 31 August 2023).

14. European Banking Authority, *EBA Report on High Earners: Data as of End of 2019*, 2021, www.eba.europa.eu/sites/default/documents/files/document_library/Publications/Reports/2021/1018449/Report%20on%20High%20Earners%202019.pdf (accessed 6 October 2022).

15. Economic Policy Institute, Inequality in annual earnings worsens in 2021, 21 December 2021, www.epi.org/publication/inequality-2021-ssa-data/#:~:text=The%20share%20of%20the%20top,of%20the%20top%200.1%25%20share. (accessed 9 July 2023).

16. High Pay Centre analysis based on AFL-CIO, Executive paywatch, 2022, https://aflcio.org/paywatch (accessed 9 July 2023).

17. *Sunday Times*, The Sunday Times Rich List 2023, 2023, www.thetimes.co.uk/sunday-times-rich-list (accessed 6 July 2023).

18. Forbes, World billionaires list, 2023, www.forbes.com/billionaires/ (accessed 20 July 2023).

19. Figures from National Lottery, All you need to know about Lotto, 2022, www.national-lottery.co.uk/games/lotto/about-lotto#What-are-the-average-jackpots-compared-with-the-previous-game (accessed 29 November 2022).

20. Based on analysis of listings on rightmove.com as of 8 October 2022.

21. *Guardian*, Russian oligarch's seized superyacht sold for $37.5m, 27 September 2022, www.theguardian.com/news/2022/sep/27/axioma-russian-oligarch-seized-superyacht-sold-gibraltar (accessed 9 October 2022).

22. Globalair.com, Helicopters for sale, 2022, www.globalair.com/aircraft-for-sale/helicopters (accessed October 9 2022).

2 The Opportunity Cost of the Super-Rich

1. CAGE, *Capital Gains and UK Inequality: CAGE Working Paper no. 465*, 2020 https://warwick.ac.uk/fac/soc/economics/research/centres/cage/manage/publications/wp465.2020.pdf (accessed 30 November 2023).
2. World Inequality Database, *Top 1% National Income Share* (2023) https://wid.world/world/#sptinc_p99p100_z/US;FR;DE;SE;BE;NL;GB/last/eu/k/p/yearly/s/false/5.086/40/curve/false/country (accessed 30 November 2023). More recent figures from the WID show the UK share falling from 14% to 10% between 2020 and 2022 but these figures are based on extrapolations and could reflect measurement challenges and fluctuations during the Covid-19 pandemic.
3. CAGE, *The UK's wealth distribution and characteristics of high-wealth households CAGE working paper no. 576* (2021), (accessed 28 November 2022).
4. World Inequality Database, *Top 1% net personal wealth share* and *Bottom 50% net personal wealth share* (2023) https://wid.world/world/#shweal_p99p100_z/US;FR;DE;SE;BE;NL;GB/last/eu/k/p/yearly/s/false/10.833/100/curve/false/country and https://wid.world/world/#shweal_pop50_z/US;FR;DE;SE;BE;NL;GB/last/eu/k/p/yearly/s/false/-2.1525/10/curve/false/country (accessed 30 November 2023).
5. UBS, *Global Wealth Report 2023*, 2023, www.ubs.com/global/en/family-office-uhnw/reports/global-wealth-report-2023.html (accessed 8 October 2023).
6. Calculations based on figure of £1.3 trillion total UK incomes extrapolated from CAGE, *Capital Gains and UK Inequality: CAGE Working Paper no. 465*, 2020 https://warwick.ac.uk/fac/soc/economics/research/centres/cage/manage/publications/wp465.2020.pdf (accessed 30 November 2023) plus 55 million UK adult population via ONS, *Estimates of the population for the UK, England, Wales, Scotland and Northern Ireland* (2022), www.ons.gov.uk/peoplepopulationandcommunity/populationandmigration/populationestimates/datasets/populationestimatesforukenglandandwalesscotlandandnorthernireland (accessed 10 October 2023).
7. Autonomy, Paying for Covid: Capping excessive salaries to save industries, 2020, https://autonomy.work/portfolio/payratios/ (accessed 13 October 2022).

8. Calculations based on income per adult of €58,951 provided by the World Income Database, an adult population of 258.3 million via United States Census Bureau (2021), U.S. Adult Population Grew Faster Than Nation's Total Population From 2010 to 2020 via www.census.gov/library/stories/2021/08/united-states-adult-population-grew-faster-than-nations-total-population-from-2010-to-2020.html (accessed 10 October 2023) and exchange rate of $1 to €0.951 based on Inland Revenue Service (2023), Yearly Average Currency Exchange Rates via www.irs.gov/individuals/international-taxpayers/yearly-average-currency-exchange-rates (accessed 10 October 2023).

9. Centre for Competitive Advantage in the Global Economy, *The UK's Wealth Distribution and Characteristics of High Wealth Households*, CAGE Working Paper 576, 2021, https://warwick.ac.uk/fac/soc/economics/research/centres/cage/manage/publications/wp576.2021.pdf (accessed 28 November 2022). The 23 per cent of total wealth of £15.1 trillion attributed to the wealthiest 1 per cent equates to £3.5 trillion.

10. There are about 27.8 million homes in Great Britain. See English Housing Survey, Section 2: Housing stock annex tables, 2022, www.gov.uk/government/statistics/english-housing-survey-2021-to-2022-headline-report www.gov.scot/publications/housing-statistics-2020-2021-key-trends-summary/pages/6/ https://statswales.gov.wales/Catalogue/Housing/Dwelling-Stock-Estimates/dwellingstockestimates-by-year-tenure (accessed 14 October 2022). Based on dwelling size of 97 square metres (average for England) this equates to just under 12,000 £5 notes (measuring 1250mm × 650mm) or £60,000 per home = £1.7 trillion across 27.8 million homes. Subtract £1.7 trillion from £3.5 trillion in total wealth = £1.8 trillion. Research paper records average wealth of £5.1m per adult for each family in the top 1 per cent based on aggregate wealth of £3.5 trillion, falling to £2.6 million if aggregate wealth were reduced by £1.7 trillion.

11. Costs based on Institute for Public Policy Research, To support low income households, it's time to reduce the cost of daily bus travel, 2022, www.ippr.org/blog/time-to-reduce-the-cost-of-daily-bus-travel (accessed 18 October 2022); Crisis, Assessing the costs and benefits of Crisis' plan to end homelessness, 2018, www.crisis.org.uk/ending-homelessness/homelessness-knowledge-hub/cost-of-homelessness/assessing-the-costs-and-benefits-of-crisis-plan-to-end-homelessness-2018/ (accessed 18 October 2022); and Gov.UK, Public spending statistics: May 2022, 2022, www.gov.uk/government/statistics/public-spending-statistics-release-may-2022/public-spending-statistics-may-2022 (accessed 18 October 2022).

12. Based on analysis of the Sunday Times Rich List, 2022 and *Credit Suisse Global Wealth Report: Raw Data Material*, 2022, and *Credit Suisse Global Wealth Report*, 2022, www.credit-suisse.com/about-us/en/reports-research/global-wealth-report/tables.html and www.credit-suisse.com/about-us/en/reports-research/global-wealth-report.html#:~:text=Global%20Wealth%20Report%202022&text=Total%20global%20wealth%20grew%20by,fastest%20annual%20rate%20ever%20recorded (accessed 9 October 2022).

13. See Action against Hunger, World hunger facts, 2022, www.actionagainsthunger.org/the-hunger-crisis/world-hunger-facts/ (accessed 26 January 2023) and Oxfam, Water and sanitation, 2023, www.oxfam.org/en/what-we-do/issues/water-and-sanitation#:~:text=2.3%20billion%20people%20lack%20access,such%20as%20toilets%20or%20latrines (accessed 26 January 2023).

14. High Pay Centre, *Pay Ratios and the FTSE 350: An Analysis of the First Disclosures*, 2020, https://highpaycentre.org/wp-content/uploads/2020/12/0.1_MUL1564-FOUNDATION-Pay-ratios-report.pdf (accessed 13 October 2022).

15. Figures based on the High Pay Centre CEO pay database, covering all FTSE 350 companies with over 250 UK employees, and relate to companies' most recent annual report as of 30 September 2022.

16. High Pay Centre, CEO pay survey 2022: CEO pay surges 39%, 22 August 2022, https://highpaycentre.org/ceo-pay-survey-2022-ceo-pay-surges-39/ (accessed 6 October 2022).

17. AFL-CIO, Company pay ratios, 2022, https://aflcio.org/paywatch/company-pay-ratios (accessed 22 July 2023).

18. AFL-CIO, Highest-paid CEOs, 2022, https://aflcio.org/paywatch/highest-paid-ceos (accessed 22 July 2023).

19. London Stock Exchange, FTSE 100, 2023, www.londonstockexchange.com/indices/ftse-100

20. High Pay Centre/Trades Union Congress, How the shareholder first business model contributes to poverty, inequality and climate change, 13 November 2019, https://highpaycentre.org/how-the-shareholder-first-business-model-contributes-to-poverty-inequality-and-climate-change/ (accessed 23 January 2023).

21. Figures via High Pay Centre/Trades Union Congress, Who benefits from returns to shareholders?, 10 January 2022, https://highpaycentre.org/who-benefits-from-returns-to-shareholders/

22. Office for National Statistics, Household total wealth in Great Britain: April 2018 to March 2020, 2022, www.ons.gov.uk/peoplepopulationandcommunity/personalandhouseholdfinances/incomeandwealth/

bulletins/totalwealthingreatbritain/april2018tomarch2020 (accessed 22 July 2022).

23. Office for National Statistics, Employee workplace pensions in the UK: 2021 provisional and 2020 final results, 2022, www.ons.gov.uk/employmentandlabourmarket/peopleinwork/workplacepensions/bulletins/annualsurveyofhoursandearningspensiontables/2021 provisionaland2020finalresults (accessed 22 July 2022).

24. High Pay Centre/Trades Union Congress, How the shareholder first business model contributes to poverty, inequality and climate change, 2019, 13 November 2019, https://highpaycentre.org/how-the-shareholder-first-business-model-contributes-to-poverty-inequality-and-climate-change/ (accessed 23 January 2023).

25. *New York Times*, Who owns stocks? Explaining the rise in inequality during the pandemic, 26 January 2021, www.nytimes.com/2021/01/26/upshot/stocks-pandemic-inequality.html (accessed 22 July 2022).

26. Harvard Business School, *Employee Ownership and Wealth Inequality: A Path to Reducing Wealth Concentration*, 2021, www.hbs.edu/ris/Publication%20Files/22-021update_2436e39f-f7ff-4883-90a3-a17cc75 b1bc1.pdf (accessed 22 July 2022).

3 The Economic Case for Equality

1. *Guardian*, Joseph Stiglitz: Tax high earners at 70 per cent to tackle widening inequality, 22 January 2023, www.theguardian.com/news/2023/jan/22/joseph-stiglitz-economist-income-tax-high-earners-70-per-cent-inequality (accessed 5 July 2023).

2. *Guardian*, IMF calls for wealth tax to help cover cost of Covid pandemic, 7 April 2021, www.theguardian.com/business/2021/apr/07/imf-wealth-tax-cost-covid-pandemic-rich-poor (accessed 5 July 2023).

3. See https://patrioticmillionaires.org/ (Patriotic Millionaires) or https://patrioticmillionaires.uk/ (Patriotic Millionaires UK) (accessed 5 July 2023).

4. *Financial Times*, Britain and the US are poor societies with some very rich people, 16 September 2022, www.ft.com/content/ef265420-45e8-497b-b308-xc951baa68945 (accessed 16 October 2022). Calculations based on *Financial Times* interactive tool, using disposable household income in 2020 dollars adjusted to achieve 'purchasing power parity' (i.e. accounting for price differences between countries). The highest threshold provided by the data source was the top 3 per cent, so it was not possible to make comparisons between the top 1 per cent in each country using the tool.

5. Stats on 'top tax rates' for the cited countries taken from OECD, Table 1.7: Top statutory personal income tax rates, 2022, https://stats.oecd.org/Index.aspx?DataSetCode=TABLE_I7 (accessed 9 January 2022).

6. Stats on 'statutory corporate tax rates' for the cited countries taken from OECD, *Corporate Tax Statistics*, 4th edn, 2022, via www.oecd.org/tax/beps/corporate-tax-statistics-database.htm (accessed 9 January 2022).

7. Data on collective bargaining coverage for the cited countries taken from European Trade Union Institute, Collective bargaining, 2022, www.worker-participation.eu/National-Industrial-Relations/Across-Europe/Collective-Bargaining2 (accessed 9 January 2022).

8. International Labor Organisation, *Working Time and Work–Life Balance Around the World*, 2023, www.ilo.org/global/publications/books/WCMS_864222/lang--en/index.htm (accessed 10 March 2023).

9. Atif Mian, Ludwig Straub and Amir Sufi, *The Saving Glut of the Rich*, NBER, 2021, https://scholar.harvard.edu/files/straub/files/mss_rich savingglut.pdf (accessed 16 January 2023).

10. Federal Reserve Bank of Boston, *Estimating the Marginal Propensity to Consume Using the Distributions of Income, Consumption, and Wealth*, Working Papers 9-14, 2019, www.bostonfed.org/publications/research-department-working-paper/2019/estimating-the-marginal-propensity-to-consume-using-the-distributions-income-consumption-wealth.aspx#:~:text=The%20marginal%20propensity%20to%20consume%20(MPC)%20is%20lower%20at%20the,it%20is%20for%20wealthy%20households. (accessed 10 September 2023).

11. Bloomberg, How the world's richest people are driving global warming, 23 March 2022, www.bloomberg.com/graphics/2022-wealth-carbon-emissions-inequality-powers-world-climate/?leadSource=uverify%20wall (accessed October 17 2022).

12. *The Conversation*, Private planes, mansions and superyachts: What gives billionaires like Musk and Abramovich such a massive carbon footprint, 16 February 2021, https://theconversation.com/private-planes-mansions-and-superyachts-what-gives-billionaires-like-musk-and-abramovich-such-a-massive-carbon-footprint-152514 (accessed October 17 2022).

13. Our World in Data, Per capita CO_2: Where do our emissions come from?, 10 June 2022, https://ourworldindata.org/emissions-by-sector (accessed 18 October 2022).

14. Crisis, 227,000 households across Britain are experiencing the worst forms of homelessness, 23 December 2021, www.crisis.org.uk/about-us/media-centre/227-000-households-across-britain-are-

experiencing-the-worst-forms-of-homelessness/ (accessed 17 October 2022).

15. Shelter, Social housing deficit, 2022, https://england.shelter.org.uk/ support_us/campaigns/social_housing_deficit (accessed 17 October 2022); Office for National Statistics, Young adults living with their parents, 2022, www.ons.gov.uk/peoplepopulationandcommunity/ birthsdeathsandmarriages/families/datasets/youngadultsliving withtheirparents (accessed 17 October 2022); and Office for National Statistics, Living longer: changes in housing tenure over time, 10 February 2020, www.ons.gov.uk/peoplepopulationandcommunity/ birthsdeathsandmarriages/ageing/articles/livinglonger/changes inhousingtenureovertime (accessed 17 October 2022).

16. Resolution Foundation, *Game of Homes: The Rise of Multiple Property Ownership in Britain*, June 2019, www.resolutionfoundation.org/app/ uploads/2019/06/Game-of-Homes.pdf (accessed 17 October 2022). Figures based on Figure 10, showing that 1.9 million own buy-to-let properties, and p. 15, noting that 1 in 10 landlords own more than three properties.

17. English Housing Survey 2018–19 Second Homes factsheet, 2020, https://assets.publishing.service.gov.uk/government/uploads/system/ uploads/attachment_data/file/898190/2020_EHS_second_homes_ factsheet.pdf (accessed October 17 2022).

18. Joseph Rowntree Foundation, *Does Income Inequality Cause Health and Social Problems?* September 2011, www.jrf.org.uk/report/does-income- inequality-cause-health-and-social-problems (accessed 27 March 2023).

19. Frontier Economics, *The UK's Net Zero Investment Gaps: A Report for E3G and WWF*, September 2022, www.e3g.org/wp-content/uploads/ Net-zero-investment-gap-22.10.26-Final-STC.pdf (accessed 10 August 2023).

20. International Monetary Fund, Cost of aging, *Finance and Development*, vol. 54, no. 1, March 2017, www.imf.org/external/pubs/ft/fandd/2017/ 03/lee.htm (accessed 10 August 2023).

21. See for example *Business Insider*, Critics say a wealth tax wouldn't work. Argentina just brought in $2.4 billion with one, 4 May 2021 www. businessinsider.com/one-time-wealth-tax-in-argentina-brought-in-24- billion-2021-5?r=US&IR=T (accessed 19 August 2023); *Merco Express*, Wealth tax returns twice as much as expected in Bolivia, 28 April 2021, https://en.mercopress.com/2021/04/28/wealth-tax-returns-twice-as- much-as-expected-in-bolivia (accessed 19 August 2023); *Majorca Daily Bulletin*, What is Spain's solidarity tax?, 28 April 2023, www. majorcadailybulletin.com/island-life/paperwork/2023/04/

28/112555/spanish-taxes-what-spain-solidarity-tax.html (accessed 19 August 2023).

22. CNN, May Day protest erupts in Paris as France seethes about a hike in the retirement age, 1 May 2023, https://edition.cnn.com/2023/05/01/europe/france-pension-protests-explainer-intl/index.html (accessed 19 August 2023).

23. University of Glasgow, Over 300,000 excess deaths in Great Britain attributed to UK government's austerity policies, 5 October 2022, www.gla.ac.uk/news/headline_885099_en.html (accessed 19 August 2023).

24. *Guardian*, Ditching two-child limit is a no-brainer. Why doesn't Labour commit to it?, 25 July 2023, www.theguardian.com/society/2023/jul/25/ditching-two-child-limit-is-a-no-brainer-why-doesnt-labour-commit-to-it (accessed 19 August 2023).

4 The Exaggerated Value of the Super-Rich

1. For OECD country tax rates, see OECD, *Taxing Wages 2022: Impact of COVID-19 on the Tax Wedge in OECD Countries*, 2022, www.oecd-ilibrary.org/taxation/taxing-wages-2022_f7f1e68a-en (accessed 28 September 2023) and OECD, *FOCUS on Top Incomes and Taxation on OECD Countries: Was the Crisis a Game Changer?*, 2014, www.oecd.org/social/OECD2014-FocusOnTopIncomes.pdf (accessed 12 April 2023).

2. London School of Economics International Inequalities Institute, *The Economic Consequences of Major Tax Cuts for the Rich*, Working Paper 55, December 2020, http://eprints.lse.ac.uk/107919/1/Hope_economic_consequences_of_major_tax_cuts_published.pdf (accessed 12 April 2023).

3. Centre for Economic Policy Research, A theory of fair pay, 27 January 2023, https://cepr.org/voxeu/columns/theory-fair-ceo-pay (accessed 3 February 2023).

4. For a selection of evidence showing how incentive pay crowds out existing intrinsic motivation for CEOs see Professor Sandy Pepper, *If You're So Ethical Why are You So Highly Paid?*, 2023, https://press.lse.ac.uk/site/books/m/10.31389/lsepress/eth/ (accessed 25 August 2023).

5. High Pay Centre, *Analysis of UK CEO pay in 2022*, August 2023, https://highpaycentre.org/wp-content/uploads/2023/08/Copy-of-CEO-pay-report-2023-1-1.pdf (accessed 31 August 2023).

6. See https://news.wpcarey.asu.edu/20220916-what-foreign-accent-says-about-ceo-investors (accessed 29 September 2023).

7. High Pay Centre, *Global CEO Appointments: A Very Domestic Issue*, 2013, https://highpaycentre.org/wp-content/uploads/2020/09/CEO_mobility_final.pdf (accessed 20 December 2022).

8. Henrik Kleven, Camille Landais, Mathilde Muñoz and Stefanie Stantcheva, Taxation and migration: Evidence and policy implications, *Journal of Economic Perspectives*, vol. 34, no. 2, 2020, https://pubs.aeaweb.org/doi/pdfplus/10.1257/jep.34.2.119 (accessed 30 January 2023).

9. IZA Institute of Labor Economics, IZA DP No. 16432: Taxation and Migration by the Super-Rich (2023) via https://docs.iza.org/dp16432.pdf (accessed 1 December 2023).

10. Tax Justice Network, 'Wealth taxes will cause the rich to flee': 12 wealth tax myths debunked, 25 May 2023, www.taxjustice.uk/blog/wealth-taxes-will-cause-the-rich-to-flee-11-wealth-tax-myths-debunked (accessed 23 August 2023).

11. LSE Public Policy Review, Is it possible to tax the super-rich?, 24 November 2022, https://ppr.lse.ac.uk/articles/10.31389/lseppr.70 (accessed 12 August 2023).

12. UN News, Ozone layer recovery is on track, due to success of Montreal Protocol, 9 January 2023, https://news.un.org/en/story/2023/01/1132277#:~:text=In%20a%20report%20published%20every,of%20banned%20ozone%2Ddepleting%20substances (accessed 20 September 2023); and OECD, International community strikes a ground-breaking tax deal for the digital age, 8 October 2021, www.oecd.org/tax/international-community-strikes-a-ground-breaking-tax-deal-for-the-digital-age.htm (accessed 20 September 2023).

13. Institute on Taxation and Economic Policy, Who pays taxes in America in 2020?, 14 July 2020, https://itep.org/who-pays-taxes-in-america-in-2020/ (accessed 15 August 2023).

14. Institute for Fiscal Studies, *Tax Revenues: Where Does the Money Come From and What are the Next Government's Challenges?*, IFS Briefing Note BN198, April 2017, https://ifs.org.uk/sites/default/files/output_url_files/BN198.pdf (accessed 15 August 2023).

15. *Sunday Times*, The Sunday Times Rich List 2023, 2023, www.thetimes.co.uk/sunday-times-rich-list and NewsUK, The Sunday Times Tax List reveals the UK's hundred biggest taxpayers, 2023, www.news.co.uk/latest-news/the-sunday-times-tax-list-reveals-uks-100-biggest-taxpayers/ (accessed 25 August 2023).

16. Atif Mian, Ludwig Straub and Amir Sufi, *The Saving Glut of the Rich*, NBER, 2021, https://scholar.harvard.edu/files/straub/files/mss_rich savingglut.pdf (accessed 16 January 2023).

17. Legal Cheek, Number of law graduates hits record high, 22 September 2022, www.legalcheek.com/2022/09/number-of-law-graduates-hits-record-high/ (accessed 19 December 2022).
18. Higher Education Statistics Authority, Table 19 – Standard industrial classification of graduates entering work in the UK by provider, 2023, www.hesa.ac.uk/data-and-analysis/graduates/table-19 (accessed 5 October 2023).
19. British Academy, *Business and Management Provision in UK Higher Education*, 2021, www.thebritishacademy.ac.uk/publications/business-and-management-provision-in-uk-higher-education/ (accessed 19 December 2021).
20. Figures for FTSE 350 executives, lawyers and accountants based on High Pay Centre analysis. High Pay Centre, *High Pay Hour 2023*, 5 January 2023, https://highpaycentre.org/high-pay-hour-how-quickly-ceos-earn-the-uk-median-wage/ (accessed 30 January 2023). Data on bankers' pay based on European Banking Authority, *EBA Report on High Earners Data as of End of 2019*, 2021, www.eba.europa.eu/sites/default/documents/files/document_library/Publications/Reports/2021/1018449/Report%20on%20High%20Earners%202019.pdf (accessed 30 January 2023).

5 Unearned Income and Wealth

1. University of Essex, *Top Incomes in the UK: Analysis of the 2015–16 Survey of Personal Incomes*, ISER Working Paper Series No. 2019-06, 2019, www.econstor.eu/bitstream/10419/200385/1/1667563858.pdf (accessed 20 February 2023).
2. Office for National Statistics, Estimates of earnings for the highest paid employee jobs by public and private sectors, UK, 26 October 2022, www.ons.gov.uk/employmentandlabourmarket/peopleinwork/earningsandworkinghours/datasets/estimatesofearningsforthehighestpaidemployeejobsbypublicandprivatesectorsuk (accessed 23 February 2023).
3. *Harvard Business Review*, How CEOs manage time, July–August 2018, https://hbr.org/2018/07/how-ceos-manage-time (accessed 20 February 2023).
4. *Sunday Times* (2023) The Sunday Times Rich List, 2023, www.thetimes.co.uk/sunday-times-rich-list (accessed September 12 2023).
5. INews, Sir James Dyson says thank you to old boarding school for his scholarship by making £19m donation, 19 July 2019, https://inews.co.uk/news/education/james-dyson-boarding-school-donation-

scholarship-greshams-tax-billionaire-303904 (accessed 7 February 2023).

6. Bloomberg, BlueCrest's Platt turns grandma's advice into hedge fund gold, 6 January 2010, www.bloomberg.com/news/articles/2010-01-06/bluecrest-s-platt-turns-grandma-s-advice-into-hedge-fund-gold?leadSource=uverify%20wall (accessed 8 February 2023).

7. Sutton Trust, *Elitist Britain 2019: The Educational Backgrounds of Britain's Leading People*, 2019, www.suttontrust.com/wp-content/uploads/2019/12/Elitist-Britain-2019.pdf (accessed 8 February 2023).

8. New Financial LLP, Book summary: The class ceiling: Why it pays to be privileged, 2022, https://newfinancial.org/wp-content/uploads/2019/07/The-Class-Ceiling-brief-summary.pdf (accessed 8 February 2023).

9. *Forbes*, The Forbes 400 self-made score: From silver spooners to bootstrappers, 8 September 2020, www.forbes.com/sites/jonathan ponciano/2020/09/08/self-made-score/ (accessed 12 September 2023).

10. CNBC, Jeff Bezos got his parents to invest nearly $250,000 in Amazon in 1995 – they might be worth $30 billion today, 2 August 2018, via www.cnbc.com/2018/08/02/how-jeff-bezos-got-his-parents-to-invest-in-amazon--turning-them-into.html; and *New Yorker*, The face of Facebook, 20 September 2010, www.newyorker.com/magazine/2010/09/20/the-face-of-facebook#:~:text=%E2%80%9CThey'd%20 come%20over%2C,prodigy%2C%E2%80%9D%20Newman%20 told%20me. (accessed 18 September 2023).

11. High Pay Centre, CEO pay survey 2022: CEO pay surges 39%, 22 August 2022, via https://highpaycentre.org/ceo-pay-survey-2022-ceo-pay-surges-39/ (accessed 12 February 2023).

12. AJ Bell, *Dividend Dashboard: Q1 2023*, January 2023, www.ajbell.co.uk/sites/default/files/AJBYI_Q1-2023_Dividend_dashboard.pdf (accessed 1 September 2023).

13. *Fortune*, Why fewer founder-CEOs run Fortune 500 companies in 2023, 5 June 2023, https://fortune.com/2023/06/05/fewer-founder-ceos-fortune-500-companies/ (accessed 13 September 2023).

14. High Pay Centre, FTSE 100 CEOs get half a million pound pay rise, 21 August 2023, https://highpaycentre.org/ftse-100-ceos-get-half-a-million-pound-pay-rise/ (accessed 31 August 2023).

15. London Stock Exchange, BAE Systems plc, 2023, www.london stockexchange.com/stock/BA./bae-systems-plc/company-page (accessed 22 September 2023).

16. London Business School, Are CEOs rewarded for luck?, 20 September 2023, www.london.edu/think/are-ceos-rewarded-for-luck (accessed 23 September 2023).

17. High Pay Centre, *Made to Measure: How Opinion about Performance Becomes Fact*, 2015, https://highpaycentre.org/wp-content/uploads/2020/09/FINAL_MADE_TO_MEASURE.pdf (accessed 18 September 2023).

18. The Financial Services Authority's report into the collapse of RBS noted that Goodwin's 'robust and assertive management style' had been a source of concern to the regulators long before the crash. *Guardian*, Fred Goodwin: FSA's history of concern over 'assertive' management style, 12 December 2009, www.theguardian.com/business/2011/dec/12/fred-goodwin-assertive-management-concerns (accessed 13 February 2023); similarly, an ex-Lehman Brothers employee described Fuld as a 'cult leader' who was 'all powerful in an executive suite surrounded by those who licked his ass all day'. *Management Today*, MT Special: How it all went wrong at Lehman, 2008, www.management today.co.uk/mt-special-went-wrong-lehman/article/858955 (accessed 13 February 2023).

19. Good Jobs First, Subsidy Tracker Parent Company Summary, 2023, https://subsidytracker.goodjobsfirst.org/parent/tesla-inc (accessed 23 September 2023).

20. *Guardian*, Without state spending there'd be no Google or Glaxo SmithKline, 22 April 2012, www.theguardian.com/commentisfree/2012/apr/22/without-state-spending-no-google-glaxosmithkline (accessed 23 September 2023).

21. Data on FTSE 100 dividends and buybacks from AJ Bell, BP's plans mean FTSE 100 share buybacks are on track to set new-all time high in 2022, 11 May 2022, www.ajbell.co.uk/articles/investmentarticles/244187/bps-plans-mean-ftse-100-share-buybacks-are-track-set-new-all (accessed 16 February 2023) and AJ Bell, *Dividend Dashboard Q2 2022*, 2022, www.ajbell.co.uk/sites/default/files/AJBYI_Q2-2022_Dividend_dashboard.pdf (accessed 16 February 2023).

22. *Guardian*, UK trade minister lobbied Brazil on behalf of oil giants, 19 November 2017, www.theguardian.com/environment/2017/nov/19/uk-trade-minister-lobbied-brazil-on-behalf-of-oil-giants (accessed 15 February 2023); and *Guardian*, Documents reveal extent of Shell and Rio Tinto lobbying in human rights case, 6 April 2014, www.theguardian.com/business/2014/apr/06/shell-rio-tinto-human-rights-nigeria-kiobel (accessed 15 February 2023).

23. *The Times*, The weapons company with influential friends at the highest level, 13 November 2016, www.thetimes.co.uk/article/the-weapons-company-with-influential-friends-at-the-highest-level-m76d6d9gsr0 (accessed 16 February 2023).

24. *Guardian*, 'National interest' halts arms corruption inquiry, 15 December 2006, www.theguardian.com/uk/2006/dec/15/saudiarabia. armstrade (accessed 20 September 2023).

25. Open Democracy, Exclusive: Weapons firms install 50 staff inside the Ministry of Defence, 27 September 2022, www.opendemocracy.net/en/dark-money-investigations/arms-companies-install-staff-inside-ministry-of-defence/ (accessed 16 February 2023).

26. Bank Underground, Who benefits from the implicit subsidy to 'too big to fail' banks?, 7 August 2015, https://bankunderground.co.uk/2015/07/08/who-benefits-from-the-implicit-subsidy-to-too-big-to-fail-banks/#:~:text=The%20expectation%20of%20such%20bailouts,as%20large%20as%20%C2%A3100bn. (accessed 15 February 2023).

27. Yahoo finance, More than 800,000 supermarket and care workers paid less than real living wage, 24 September 2021, https://uk.finance.yahoo.com/news/more-than-800000-supermarket-care-workers-paid-less-than-real-living-wage-113528564.html (accessed 16 February 2023).

28. Aston University, Who won? Who lost? The distributional impact of COVID-19 government support for business, 5 May 2023, https://highpaycentre.org/who-won-who-lost-the-distributional-impact-of-covid-19-government-support-for-business/ (accessed 20 September 2023).

29. *Financial Times*, Top Patisserie Valerie bosses made £2.9m from bonus scheme shares, 19 October 2018, www.ft.com/content/22214d1c-d3b3-11e8-a9f2-7574db66bcd5 (accessed 13 February 2023).

30. *Daily Mirror*, The Thomas Cook bosses who received £30million in bonuses as company collapses, 23 September 2019, www.mirror.co.uk/news/uk-news/thomas-cook-bosses-who-received-20148924 (accessed 13 February 2023).

31. People Management, Anger as Carillion bosses share £4m bonuses despite liquidation, 16 January 2018, www.peoplemanagement.co.uk/article/1742850/carillion-bosses-share-bonuses#:~:text=The%20company's%20interim%20chief%20executive,%C2%A3425%2C000%20until%20the%20summer (accessed 13 February 2023).

32. For a summary of the Thomas Cook executives' testimony to the Select Committee see *Guardian*, Thomas Cook's former bosses criticised; Boeing and Caterpillar profits fall – business live, 23 October 2019, www.theguardian.com/business/live/2019/oct/23/markets-growth-worries-brexit-uncertainty-thomas-cook-business-live?page=with:block-5db05d028f0898437061b4b7 (accessed 16 February 2023).

33. For example, see Bob Diamond, CEO of Barclays, claiming he was only made aware of the LIBOR manipulation shortly before the story broke

in the media. *Daily Telegraph*, Bob Diamond questioned by MPs on Barclays Libor scandal: as it happened, 4 July 2012, www.telegraph.co. uk/finance/newsbysector/banksandfinance/9374516/Bob-Diamond-questioned-by-MPs-on-Barclays-Libor-scandal-as-it-happened.html (accessed 15 February 2023). Or see News Corp chief executive Rebekah Brooks, who said she didn't know who journalist Glenn Mulcaire was until his arrest for phone hacking, and was unaware her organisation was paying him £92,000. *Sydney Morning Herald*, Rebekah Brooks 'didn't know' phone hacking was illegal, 26 February 2014, www.smh.com.au/world/rebekah-brooks-didnt-know-phone-hacking-was-illegal-20140226-hvdva.html (accessed 16 February 2023).

34. Sky News, Boss of British Gas owner says there is 'no excuse' after prepay meters forced on vulnerable people, 2 February 2023, https:// news.sky.com/story/british-gas-suspends-force-fitting-prepayment-meters-as-unacceptable-allegations-emerge-12801126 (accessed 30 April 2023).

35. MSCI, *Are CEOs Paid for Performance? Evaluating the Effectiveness of Equity Incentives*, July 2016, www.msci.com/documents/10199/91a7f92b-d4ba-4d29-ae5f-8022f9bb944d (accessed 12 February 2023).

36. Incomes Data Services, *Executive Remuneration in the FTSE 350 – A Focus on Performance-related Pay*, October 2014, https://highpaycentre. org/wp-content/uploads/2020/09/IDS_report_for_HPC_2014_final_211014.pdf (accessed 4 October 2023).

37. High Pay Centre, Why champions of free markets should worry about executive pay, ch. 2 in J.R. Shackleton, *Top Dogs and Fat Cats: The Debate on High Pay*, 2019, https://highpaycentre.org/wp-content/uploads/2020/08/Shackleton-Top-Dogs-Chap-2.pdf (accessed 5 October 2023).

38. CEO pay based on High Pay Centre analysis of FTSE 100 CEO pay awards in 2022. Earnings at the 99th percentile via Office for National Statistics, Estimates of earnings for the highest paid employee jobs by public and private sectors, UK, 2022, www.ons.gov.uk/employment andlabourmarket/peopleinwork/earningsandworkinghours/datasets/ estimatesofearningsforthehighestpaidemployeejobsbypublicand privatesectorsuk (accessed 10 October 2023). Calculations based on High Pay Centre analysis as of January 2023.

39. *Sunday Times*, The Sunday Times Rich List 2023, 2023, www.thetimes. co.uk/sunday-times-rich-list (accessed September 12 2023).

40. *Forbes*, Forbes 400, 27 September 2023, www.forbes.com/profile/elon-musk/?list=forbes-400 (accessed 12 September 2023); American Heart Association, How much sugar is too much?, no date, www.heart.org/ en/healthy-living/healthy-eating/eat-smart/sugar/how-much-sugar-

is-too-much (accessed 17 September 2023); Centre for Disease Control and Prevention, Adult obesity facts, no date, www.cdc.gov/obesity/data/adult.html (accessed 17 September 2023).

41. See, for example, *The Mirror*, Amazon workers 'treated like slaves and robots' as ambulances called to centres 971 times, 24 November 2023, www.mirror.co.uk/news/uk-news/amazon-workers-treated-like-slaves-25531239 and Reveal, Tesla says its factory is safer. But it left injuries off the books, 16 April 2018, https://revealnews.org/article/tesla-says-its-factory-is-safer-but-it-left-injuries-off-the-books/ (accessed 18 September 2023).

42. See, for example, *Guardian*, Facebook aware of Instagram's harmful effect on teenage girls, leak reveals, 1 September 2021, www.theguardian.com/technology/2021/sep/14/facebook-aware-instagram-harmful-effect-teenage-girls-leak-reveals (accessed 18 September 2023).

43. UN PRI, Schroders: Quantifying social and environmental impact, 18 February 2022, www.unpri.org/listed-equity/schroders-quantifying-social-and-environmental-impact/9524.article (accessed 10 September 2023).

44. Figures for companies taken from High Pay Centre analysis compiled at High Pay Centre, UK pay database, 2023, https://highpaycentre.org/uk-pay-database/ (accessed 23 February 2023).

45. According to the Essex University research, 'Financial, Insurance and Real Estate' professionals account for around 19 per cent of the richest 1 per cent by income, and around 36 per cent of the richest 0.01%.

46. UNCTAD, *Global Trade and Development Report 2022*, 2022, https://unctad.org/system/files/official-document/tdr2022_en.pdf (accessed 28 February 2023). The report acknowledges that limited speculative activity can benefit food producers and consumers by increasing liquidity and information in the markets, but suggests that the ideal ratio is around 30 per cent of market share relative to actual producers' and suppliers' 'commercial hedging' (e.g. agreeing to buy/sell a commodity at a fixed price in the future to achieve a degree of certainty, as opposed to merely betting that the price will go up or down). However, the ratio is more like 80 per cent today. This has the effect of dramatically amplifying price movements as speculators buy or sell commodities based on their future expectations.

47. *Daily Mail*, Pandemic plunderers scandal: Private equity buy-up of High Street firms during lockdown has cost 40,000 jobs, 25 May 2021, www.dailymail.co.uk/news/article-9618579/Pandemic-High-Street-buy-firms-lockdown-cost-40-000-staff-jobs.html; and *Daily Mail*, Ten deals to make your blood boil: Care homes in crisis, defence firms

stripped, and even vet bills sent soaring. How the private equity barons wrought havoc in British buy-ups, 24 May 2021, www.dailymail.co.uk/news/article-9614377/Ten-deals-make-blood-boil-private-equity-barons-wrought-havoc-British-buy-ups.html (all accessed 28 February 2023). Specific practices criticised include the substantial management fees charged by the private equity owners of British Steel, having bought the company for £1; the £1.2 billion dividends paid to private equity firms invested in Debenhams prior to the firm's collapse; and the care home chain Southern Cross, which collapsed six years after being sold by a private equity firm for £600 million.

48. The Kay Review of UK equity markets concluded in 2012 that the volume of short-term 'trading' in the UK exceeded the core level needed to support liquidity and could mostly be considered a zero-sum game between traders seeking to make gains at each other's expense, while encouraging companies to overly focus on short-term performance. Gov.uk, *The Kay Review of UK Equity Markets and Long-term Decision Making*, July 2012, https://assets.publishing.service.gov.uk/government/uploads/system/uploads/attachment_data/file/253454/bis-12-917-kay-review-of-equity-markets-final-report.pdf (accessed 28 February 2023). Critics of short selling include an analysis by a Columbia University professor who found that 86 per cent of pseudonymous posts on a leading financial website attacking a particular company were preceded by suspiciously high number of 'short' trades that would profit from a decline in the company's value. Joshua Mitts, Short and distort, 49 *Journal of Legal Studies*, 287, 2020, https://scholarship.law.columbia.edu/faculty_scholarship/2782/ (accessed 28 February 2023).

49. Figures from Good Jobs First, *Violation Tracker UK*, 2023, https://violationtrackeruk.goodjobsfirst.org/ (accessed 23 February 2023).

50. Figures from Good Jobs First, *Violation Tracker*, 2023, https://violationtracker.goodjobsfirst.org/?company_op=starts&company=&penalty_op=%3E&penalty=&offense_group=&case_category=&govt_level=&agency_code_st%5B%5D=&major_industry%5B%5D=financial+services&pres_term=&case_type=&free_text=&hq_id=&state=&order=parent_name&sort=asc&page=2 (accessed 17 September 2023).

6 How to Abolish the Super-Rich

1. Office for National Statistics, The effects of taxes and benefits on income inequality: 1977 to financial year ending 2015, 8 April 2016, www.ons.gov.uk/peoplepopulationandcommunity/personaland

householdfinances/incomeandwealth/bulletins/theeffectsoftaxes
andbenefitsonincomeinequality/1977tofinancialyearending2015
(accessed 1 March 2023).

2. Section 172 of the Companies Act 2006 (accessed 15 November 2022).

3. Trades Union Congress, *Workers' Voice in Corporate Governance: A European Perspective*, September 2015, www.tuc.org.uk/sites/default/files/WorkersVoiceinCorporateGovernance.pdf (accessed 15 November 2022).

4. The index uses measures of both formal rights and the extent of participation on three levels: in the board, at the establishment level and through collective bargaining. Available via European Trade Union Institute, European Participation Index, 2022, https://european participationindex.eu/#EPI_Countries (accessed 15 November 2022).

5. Institute for Public Policy Research, *Power to the People: How Stronger Unions can Deliver Economic Justice*, 2018, www.ippr.org/files/2018-06/cej-trade-unions-may18-.pdf (accessed 15 November 2022).

6. International Labor Organization, *Social Dialogue Report 2022: Collective Bargaining for an Inclusive, Sustainable and Resilient Recovery*, 2022, www.ilo.org/wcmsp5/groups/public/---dgreports/---dcomm/---publ/documents/publication/wcms_842807.pdf (accessed 16 November 2022).

7. US Department of the Treasury, Labor unions and the US economy, 28 August 2023, https://home.treasury.gov/news/featured-stories/labor-unions-and-the-us-economy (accessed 19 September 2023).

8. Economic Policy Institute, *Fear at Work*, report, 23 July 2020, www.epi.org/publication/fear-at-work-how-employers-scare-workers-out-of-unionizing/ (accessed 20 September 2023).

9. New Zealand Legislation, Employment Relations Act 2000, www.legislation.govt.nz/act/public/2000/0024/latest/DLM58646.html (accessed 19 September 2023).

10. Congressman Bobby Scott, Bipartisan labor leaders introduce bill to protect workers' right to organize, 28 February 2023, https://bobbyscott.house.gov/media-center/press-releases/bipartisan-labor-leaders-introduce-bill-protect-workers-right-organize (accessed 19 September 2023).

11. Trades Union Congress, *Raising Pay for Everyone*, 23 August 2023, www.tuc.org.uk/research-analysis/reports/raising-pay-everyone (accessed 19 September 2023).

12. Employee Ownership Association, The Employee Ownership Top 50 2022, 2022, www.rm2.co.uk/resources/eo-top-50/employee-ownership-top-50-2022/ (accessed 14 November 2022).

13. *Harvard Business Review*, The big benefits of employee ownership, 13 May 2021, https://hbr.org/2021/05/the-big-benefits-of-employee-ownership (accessed 30 August 2023).

14. Commonwealth, *Examining the Inclusive Ownership Fund*, 2019, www.common-wealth.co.uk/reports/examining-the-inclusive-ownership-fund (accessed 15 November 2022).

15. *White & Case*, Value-sharing within a company: Upcoming changes, 7 April 2023, www.whitecase.com/insight-alert/value-sharing-within-company-upcoming-changes (accessed 19 September 2023).

16. National Bureau of Economic Research, The Effect of Mandatory Profit Sharing on workers and firms: Evidence from France (2023) https://www.nber.org/papers/w31804#:~:text=Since%201967%2C%20all%20French%20firms,pre%2Dtax%20income%20to%20workers. (accessed 30 November 2023).

17. CBS News, How would you feel about a 94 per cent tax rate?, 7 December 2011, www.cbsnews.com/news/how-would-you-feel-about-a-94-tax-rate/ (accessed 29 November 2022).

18. Inequality.org, From the Wall Street Journal: A deeply flawed CEO pay analysis, 2 August 2022, https://inequality.org/great-divide/flawed-ceo-pay-analysis/ (accessed 29 November 2022) and *New York Times*, Can we close the pay gap?, 29 March 2014, https://archive.nytimes.com/opinionator.blogs.nytimes.com/2014/03/29/can-we-close-the-pay-gap/ (accessed 29 November 2022).

19. John Lewis Partnership, Terms of reference for the Remuneration Committee of the Board of John Lewis Partnership plc, 15 July 2021, www.johnlewispartnership.co.uk/content/dam/cws/pdfs/about-us/governance/remunerations-comittee-tor.pdf (accessed 20 September 2023).

20. Christian Aid, How Christian Aid pays its staff, 10 February 2020, www.christianaid.org.uk/resources/our-work/how-christian-aid-pays-its-staff#:~:text=For%20salaries%20of%20staff%20based,4%3A1%20on%20UK%20salaries (accessed 20 September 2023).

21. *Guardian*, San Francisco voters approve new taxes for wealthy CEOs and tech companies, 5 November 2020, www.theguardian.com/us-news/2020/nov/05/san-francisco-voters-approve-new-taxes-wealthy-ceos-tech-companies (accessed 20 September 2023).

22. Wealth Tax Commission, Tax simulator, 2023, http://taxsimulator.ukwealth.tax/#/ (accessed 2 May 2023).

23. Centre for Competitive Advantage in the Global Economy/LSE Inequalities Institute, Reforms to the taxation of wealth, 2022, https://arunadvani.com/taxreform.html (accessed 18 November 2022).

24. Centre for Competitive Advantage in the Global Economy, *Fixing National Insurance: A Better Way to Fund Social Care*, Policy Briefing 33, September 2021, https://warwick.ac.uk/fac/soc/economics/research/centres/cage/manage/publications/bn33.2021.pdf (accessed 12 March 2023).

25. *Boston Review*, Class and inequality: Taxing the super rich, 17 March 2020, www.bostonreview.net/forum/gabriel-zucman-taxing-superrich/ (accessed 9 October 2023).

Conclusion

1. Twitter, Day 1 of General Election: Extraordinary insight from a Labour MP. No billionaires in Britain, 31 October 2019, https://twitter.com/Emmabarnett/status/1189863151598260233 (accessed 6 March 2023).

2. Figure derived from jackpots over the previous 180 days listed on the National Lottery website – Lottery.co.uk, Lotto statistics, 2023, www.lottery.co.uk/lotto/statistics (accessed 15 March 2023).

3. Resolution Foundation, British workers are living through a two-decade wage stagnation costing £15,000, 18 November 2022, www.resolutionfoundation.org/press-releases/british-workers-are-living-through-a-two-decade-wage-stagnation-costing-15000/ (accessed March 6 2023).

4. World Bank, GDP per capita, PPP (constant 2017 international $) – United Kingdom, United States, Germany, 2023, https://data.worldbank.org/indicator/NY.GDP.PCAP.PP.KD?end=2022&locations=GB-US-DE&start=2008 (accessed 6 October 2023).

5. OECD, Income inequality, 2023, https://data.oecd.org/inequality/income-inequality.htm (accessed 6 March 2023).

6. International Monetary Fund, Government expenditure, percent of GDP, 2022, www.imf.org/external/datamapper/exp@FPP/USA/FRA/GBR/SWE/ESP/ITA/DNK/BEL/DEU/NLD/NOR/CHE/FIN/IRL/PRT/AUT

7. Our World in Data, Government spending. Figure: Public social spending as a share of GDP, 1880 to 2016, 2023, https://ourworldindata.org/government-spending (accessed March 6 2023).

8. World Inequality Database, Figure: Income inequality in the United Kingdom, 2023, https://wid.world/country/united-kingdom/ (accessed 19 September 2023).

9. World Inequality Database, Income inequality in the USA and Wealth inequality in the USA, 2023, https://wid.world/country/usa/ (accessed 19 September 2023).

Thanks to our Patreon subscriber:

Ciaran Kane

Who has shown generosity and comradeship in support of our publishing.

Check out the other perks you get by subscribing to our Patreon – visit patreon.com/plutopress.

Subscriptions start from £3 a month.

The Pluto Press Newsletter

Hello friend of Pluto!

Want to stay on top of the best radical books
we publish?

Then sign up to be the first to hear about our
new books, as well as special events,
podcasts and videos.

You'll also get 50% off your first order with us
when you sign up.

Come and join us!

Go to bit.ly/PlutoNewsletter